The Law of Soviet Territorial Waters

The Law of Soviet Territorial Waters

A CASE STUDY OF MARITIME LEGISLATION AND PRACTICE

William E. Butler

FREDERICK A. PRAEGER, Publishers
New York · Washington · London

The purpose of the Praeger Special Studies is to make specialized research monographs in U.S. and international economics and politics available to the academic, business, and government communities. For further information, write to the Special Projects Division, Frederick A. Praeger, Publishers, 111 Fourth Avenue, New York, N.Y. 10003.

FREDERICK A. PRAEGER, PUBLISHERS
111 Fourth Avenue, New York, N.Y. 10003, U.S.A.
77-79 Charlotte Street, London W.1, England

Published in the United States of America in 1967
by Frederick A. Praeger, Inc., Publishers

Library of Congress Catalog Card Number: 68-12380

Printed in the United States of America

TO MY FATHER AND MOTHER

PREFACE

For the importance of this study to current events one need look no further than the front page of the daily newspaper. From 1965-67: A United States Coast Guard icebreaker on an oceanographic voyage in the Kara Sea is harassed and forced to turn back by Soviet naval and air forces, the incident provoking diplomatic notes and protests; the Soviet Union again proposes the Baltic Sea be closed to warships of noncontiguous states; the masters of Russian fishing trawlers arrested and fined for violating the American twelve-mile fishing zone face disciplinary action upon their return home; Japanese fishermen are periodically arrested for violating the regime of Soviet territorial waters; American and Soviet warships are involved in brushing incidents in the Sea of Japan, a body of water Soviet publicists deem to be a regional sea; a war breaks out in the Near East over the legal status of the Gulf of Aqaba and Strait of Tiran, water routes which in geographic configuration and historical tradition are closely analogous to seas washing Soviet coasts; the Soviet Union announces the opening of the Northern Sea Route, and Japan is one of the first states to negotiate an agreement to use the Route; the Soviet Union campaigns strenuously for expanded foreign trade, a development which will entail increased contact by foreigners with the legal regime of Soviet territorial waters.

Although less on the journalistic side, it is also true that Soviet international law has not received sufficient attention from Western lawyers. Most studies have focused upon ideological and political issues; case studies of Soviet legislation and practice are few indeed. Literature in English on the international legal aspects of Soviet maritime policy is confined to a handful of topical articles, many published in the 1930's. Apart from some excellent nonlegal analyses of Soviet policies in the Arctic, little is known about the system of normative acts governing Soviet internal and territorial waters or the doctrinal innovations of Soviet international lawyers. As this study points out, there have been and are significant, even creative, differences of opinion among Soviet lawyers with respect to international legal questions which can have an impact on Soviet state practice, Soviet positions in maritime disputes with other states, and the Soviet approach to the study of international law in general.

Thus, this book is intended as a resource volume for those professionally interested in specific aspects of Soviet maritime or international law and as a case study for those concerned with the more academic question of the nexus among law, policy, and ideology.

The book describes the existing legal regime of Soviet territorial waters, outlines its pattern of development in Soviet legislation and treaty practice, and surveys its philosophical and legal foundations as they have been conceived by Soviet publicists. Chapter 1 provides a brief historical and geographical introduction to Soviet maritime policy and a rather extensive precis of Russian legislation and state practice. The regime of internal waters, with special reference to historic bays and seas, is discussed in the second chapter. A subject unique to Soviet international law, the theory of the closed sea and its various formulations, is presented in Chapter 3. The fourth Chapter examines general problems of legal terminology and defines territorial waters and manner of calculating the extent of those waters. Chapters 5, 6, and 7 explore the various kinds of jurisdiction the Soviet Union exercises over foreign vessels and nationals by way of innocent passage, criminal and civil jurisdiction, customs, sanitary inspection, salvage rules, pilot services, hot pursuit, and others. The eighth Chapter, a sea-by-sea survey around the borders of the Soviet Union, brings out special problems connected with the application of general legal norms to individual seas.

A determined effort has been made to examine and analyze all of the relevant Soviet statutory and treaty materials, diplomatic correspondence, and court decisions. Many are extremely difficult to locate and have never been available in English. Those of greatest import have been collected and translated in the documentary appendixes. A bibliography of books and articles in Russian, English, and other languages completes the volume.

The author is responsible for translations from the Russian unless indicated otherwise. Precision of expression is preferable to a literary rendering in a study of this kind, so the original Russian has been followed as literally as possible in matters of syntax and terminology. The Library of Congress transliteration scheme has been employed, except that diacritical markings, hard signs, and soft signs have been omitted. Materials in the notes are cited in the customary legal form; a full citation will be found in the bibliography.

This volume is a substantially revised and enlarged version of a study originally submitted to the Seminar on International Law Problems conducted by Professor R. R. Baxter at the Harvard Law School. In June 1966 the study was awarded the Addison Brown Prize, established in 1914 at the Harvard Law School "to be awarded annually or biennially for the best essay by one of the students in the Law School on some subject of Maritime or Private International Law. . ." The author is grateful to Professor Baxter for his many valuable comments and suggestions on the original manuscript and for encouraging revision of the study for publication.

I am also greatly indebted to Professor Harold J. Berman of the Harvard Law School, who originally stimulated my interest in Soviet law and who afforded the best possible exposure to the field by retaining me as his research assistant for two years.

Mrs. Maryllis Bartlett painstakingly and expertly typed the final copy, making a difficult task seem easy.

Finally, I must express my deep gratitude to my wife and son for coexisting with Soviet territorial waters in unfailing good humor and understanding.

Items 2-6 and 9-12 of the documentary appendixes were initially translated for <u>Soviet Statutes and Decisions</u>. They are reproduced here, some slightly revised, with the permission and by the courtesy of Mr. Myron E. Sharpe of the International Arts and Sciences Press.

William E. Butler

Washington, D. C.
August 1967

CONTENTS

Page

ABBREVIATIONS

BFSP	British and Foreign State Papers
Dokumenty	Dokumenty vneshnei politiki SSSR (Documents of USSR Foreign Policy)
For. Rel. U.S.	Foreign Relations of the United States
IM	Izveshcheniia moreplavateliam (Notices to Mariners)
LNTS	League of Nations Treaty Series
N.R.G.	Nouveau Recueil general de traites, 3d series, 40 volumes (1909-1943)
Polnoe sobranie	Polnoe sobranie zakonov rossisskoi imperii s 1649 goda (Complete Collected Laws of the Russian Empire Since 1649)
Recueil	Recueil de traites, 8 vols. (1761-1808)
RSFSR	Russian Soviet Federated Socialist Republic
SDD	Sbornik deistvuiushchikh dogovorov, soglashenii i konventsii zakliuchennykh SSSR s inostrannym gosudarstvami (Collected Treaties, Agreements, and Conventions in Force Concluded by the USSR with Foreign States)
SP SSSR	Sobranie postanovlenii soveta ministrov SSSR (Collected Decrees of the USSR Council of Ministers)
SU RSFSR	Sobranie uzakonenii i rasporiazhenii RSFSR (Collected Laws and Decrees of the RSFSR)
SZ SSSR	Sobranie zakonov i rasporiazhenii SSSR (Collected Laws and Decrees of the USSR)

U.N.	United Nations
UNTS	United Nations Treaty Series
USSR	Union of Soviet Socialist Republics
Vedomosti SSSR	Vedomosti verkhovnogo soveta SSSR (Gazette of the Supreme Soviet of the USSR)
Yb. Int'l L. Comm.	Yearbook of the International Law Commission

The Law of Soviet Territorial Waters

CHAPTER 1 GEOGRAPHIC AND HISTORICAL BACKGROUND

The territorial land mass of the Union of Soviet Socialist Republics covers one sixth of the earth's habitable surface, stretching from Eastern Europe across Northern Asia and occupying the core of the Eurasian continent. Despite a "heartland" location and 36,000 miles of frontier (27,000 miles of which are sea), the Soviet Union remains dependent upon a few vulnerable straits for maritime intercourse with the rest of the world. The fourteen seas washing the shores of the USSR provide indirect access to three oceans. Since nearly all of the Soviet coastline freezes for varying periods each year, the search for "warm-water" ports has been a vital political and economic factor in Russian and Soviet history and diplomacy.

Historically, the sea cannot be said to have played the role in Russian development that it did with the English, the Scandinavians, or the Dutch, nor even to have been as important as the rivers of Russia.[1] Several elements have interacted to influence the course and pattern of the boundaries and the regime of Soviet territorial waters.[2] The foremost of these is national security. All of the seas bordering the Soviet Union have narrow entrances which can be commanded easily by hostile foreign powers. During the Russian revolution and subsequent Civil War, allied vessels in the Baltic and the Dardanelles restricted to an uncomfortable extent the freedom of action of the Soviet Government. Indeed, it is difficult to overestimate the extent to which the presence of Allied ships restrained Bolshevik ambitions of expansion and secured the independence of nations in Eastern Europe.[3] Soviet weakness in the Baltic theater was a major factor in determining Soviet policy toward Finland and the Baltic states during the 1939-41 period, and the proximity of naval forces of the North Atlantic Treaty Organization to the Baltic continues to evoke Soviet proposals to close the sea to nonlittoral states. Similarly, the Soviet Union was compelled to endure Turkish violations of the Montreux Convention on the Turkish Straits during World War II while its Black Sea fleet was immobilized.[4] The Pacific Coast seas and the Atlantic and Pacific approaches to the Arctic seas also are susceptible to a blockade by hostile powers. Even the Arctic seas themselves, once regarded as an unguarded but impregnable frozen boundary, have become important strategically because Soviet warships can be transferred from east to west, sailing solely in Soviet-controlled seas. With the development of nuclear submarines the Arctic has become unexpectedly vulnerable. In defending a twelve-mile breadth for territorial waters, Soviet jurists have observed that the effectiveness of an attack by a nuclear submarine depends to a meaningful degree upon the proximity of the submarine to shore.[5]

Economic considerations have been a second important element. The great majority of Soviet exports and imports leave and arrive by sea. Much of the Russian merchant marine was destroyed in World War I; most of the remainder was seized by the White Armies. The resulting dependence on foreign shipping and the desperate need for imported industrial commodities from the West "account in general for the warm attitude of the Soviet state toward the rules applied by bourgeois states."[6] The nationalization of land, waters, and their resources coupled with an emphasis on the doctrine of state sovereignty encouraged Soviet jurists to regard coastal waters as an exclusively national resource. Fishing is the sixth largest industry of the Soviet Union. A total of 30 per cent of the annual catch comes from Soviet seas. On several occasions the Tsarist Government attempted to reserve exclusive fishing and hunting privileges in broad expanses of the sea. Many of the early Soviet decrees governing coastal waters were motivated by economic considerations of protecting socialist ownership.[7] This concern has continued to be reflected in Soviet postwar fishing legislation and treaties with other states.

A third element has been historical discoveries, explorations, and conquests.[8] Russians settled along the White Sea at least nine centuries ago. But the Black, Baltic, Azov, Aral, and Caspian Seas have come under partial Russian control only since about 1700. Although the Pacific shores began to be colonized late in the seventeenth century, effective Russian control of the coastal region dates from the second half of the nineteenth century. Exploration and settlement of the Arctic coasts by Russians dates to at least the thirteenth century and possibly earlier. However, inaccessibility of sources and relative unfamiliarity with the Russian language have relegated the travel accounts of Russian explorers to comparative obscurity in contrast to the well-known exploits of those hardy English and Dutch entrepreneurs who, while searching for a northeast passage, stumbled onto Muscovy. The deep and abiding interest in travel literature in West Europe and the United States has been accompanied by meticulous documentation of even the most remote voyages; Russia has had no counterpart to the Hakluyt Society. Nonetheless, Russian and Soviet explorers have engaged in pioneering expeditions which have been advanced as the basis of Soviet claims to large expanses of coastal waters.

TERRITORIAL WATERS OF THE RUSSIAN EMPIRE

Prerevolutionary Russian jurists derived the great majority of their legal doctrines from the West, including in general, their views on the juridical nature and the breadth of territorial waters. Many jurists, and often Russian state practice, supported an extension of state sovereignty over territorial waters beyond the customary three-mile limit.

Perhaps the most influential "school" was led by F. F. Martens, who defined the territorial sea as "that part of the sea which washes a possession of the coastal state and which is deemed the property of the state, and is considered an extension of the coastal territory and subject to its authority."[9] This view was also held by Zakharov,[10] Kamarovskii,[11] and Ulianitskii.[12] A somewhat middle ground was adopted by P. Kazanskii,[13] who believed the territorial sea was both a possession of the littoral state and a part of the open sea; thus, the littoral state possessed only limited authority over territorial waters. P. Sivers and A. N. Stoianov adhered to the more orthodox Western opinion that territorial waters were part of the high seas, and, consequently, the littoral state was entitled to exert only limited sovereignty.[14]

The breadth of territorial waters claimed varied with the particular interest Russia wished to protect. Of the major eighteenth and nineteenth century maritime powers, Russia was the most dissatisfied with the three-mile rule. In general, the seal fisheries were the greatest influence on Russia's claim to vast territorial waters.

The first apparent Russian assertion of a territorial sea, employing the cannon shot rule, occurred in treaties concluded with France on December 31, 1786 (Art. 28);[15] the Kingdom of the Two Sicilies on January 6, 1787 (Art. 19);[16] and with Portugal on December 9, 1787 (Art. 24).[17] On December 31, 1787, the cannon shot rule was incorporated into Russian legislation which regulated privateering.[18] An edict of Alexander I on September 4, 1821,[19] endeavored to reserve sealing and fishing regions exclusively for Russia by claiming a 100-mile belt in the Bering Sea. After strenuous objections by Great Britain and the United States, the edict was repealed in 1824. It remained, however, an example invariably cited by Russian jurists as an unjustified extension of territorial waters.

Though Russia recognized the cannon shot rule, it rejected the three-mile limit as a general rule of international law. Vice Chancellor Nesselrode protested to Great Britain on March 10, 1837, against the three-mile limit in connection with the seizure of the "Lord Ch. Spenser" in the Black Sea: "Each state reserves the right . . . to resolve this question (limit of territorial waters) in accordance with its own convenience and interests."[20] During the 1840's, Russian trading officials urged their Government to extend territorial waters to forty Italian miles in order to reduce the competition of foreign whalers. The Russian Government declined to do so, stating that protests would result "since no clear and uniform agreement has yet been arrived at among nations in regard to the limits of jurisdiction at sea."[21]

The three-mile limit was accepted for certain purposes. In 1853 instructions were issued to Russian cruisers to enforce a three-mile limit off the shores of Russian America.[22] The Russian Code of Prize Law of 1869 and the Customs Code of 1892 each provided for a three-mile limit for their respective purposes. In 1874 Britain, through the medium of a circular letter, endeavored to bring about consensus on the three-mile limit. In its reply Russia agreed that the three-mile limit was supported by practice but considered the legal view unsettled.[23]

Russian jurists advocated the cannon shot rule, pointing to its flexibility as the range of artillery increased. F. F. Martens rejected the three-mile rule as a "general obligatory law" and suggested a ten-mile limit would be more in consonance with artillery capabilities.[24] A Draft Statute on Russian Territorial Waters, proposed by an inter-departmental government commission which was chaired by Martens, recommended the cannon shot rule with a minimum limit of six miles except where otherwise established by international decree or treaty or long undisputed usage.[25] Another committee appointed in 1906 recommended a twenty-mile limit along the Murmansk coast be established and that portions of the White and Kara Seas be closed.[26]

This multiplicity of views in reality gave Russia an indefinite position on the extent of territorial waters. Early in the twentieth century steps were taken to clarify territorial limits. A decree of December 10, 1909, established a customs belt and subjected "every vessel" to supervision which was within twelve miles of shore.[27] The twelve-mile limit was incorporated into rules regulating fishing in the Priamur Guberniia (Pacific Coast) region on May 29, 1911,[28] and in a General Statute on Fishing adopted by the State Council in May 1913; the statute never became law.

These decrees were strenuously protested by Great Britain and Japan. In reply to the Japanese protest in a note sent early in 1911, the Russian Ministry of Foreign Affairs declared

> . . . in modern international law there exists no generally accepted rule concerning the limits of territorial waters within which sovereign state authority may be exercised.
>
> The question has been given widely different solutions either by international treaties or the municipal laws of a state, and very often in an unequal manner for the various protected interests (customs regulations, fisheries,

criminal or civil jurisdiction, sanitary observations, etc.)

Thus an examination of the laws dealing with the question shows that a great many States in Europe and America exercise undisputed jurisdiction within limits that exceed the so-called ordinary zone of three nautical miles. . . .

Taking into consideration the . . . provisions of laws against which no State appears to have protested, together with the fact that Russia is not bound by any international treaty fixing the 3-marine-mile zone for the territorial waters and that therefore its area cannot be measured from the viewpoint of international law except by the range of the cannons on the coast (which now even exceed the 12-nautical-mile limit) the Imperial Government is unable to admit that the Russian law of December 10, 1909, conflicts with international law.

Lastly, the Imperial Ministry deems it its duty to recall to the Japanese Embassy's memory that the Institute of International Law (whose authority on such questions is unquestionable) did not hesitate to declare (as far back as 17 years ago, when it met at Paris, in 1894) that the "usually adopted" distance of three miles was absolutely insufficient.[29]

The expansive conception of state jurisdiction over territorial waters and the twelve-mile limit held by the Russian Government and many Russian jurists found ready acceptance with the young Soviet regime. A. N. Nikolaev contended that the Soviet Government inherited the twelve-mile limit by rule of state succession.[30] A decree of the Soviet Government of May 24, 1921, extended the twelve-mile fishing limit to the White Sea and the northern Arctic seas.[31] Whether Russia and the Soviet Union had successfully asserted a twelve-mile belt of territorial waters or had asserted a three-mile belt with specialized contiguous zones of twelve miles became a controversial question in Soviet jurisprudence during the 1930's and 1940's.

NOTES

1. Sumner, A Short History of Russia 239 (1949). Some historians consider the sea to be a major driving force of Russian expansion. See Kerner, The Urge to the Sea (1946).

2. See Hartingh, Les Conceptions Soviétiques du Droit de la Mer (1960), which received a warm review in 1960 Sovetskoe gosudarstvo i pravo (Soviet State and Law), No.10, pp. 134-135.

3. Grzybowski, "The Soviet Doctrine of Mare Clausum and Policies in Black and Baltic Seas," 14 Journal of Central European Affairs 339-353 (1955).

4. See Vasilev, O turetskom "neitralitete" vo vtoroi mirovoi voine (On Turkish "Neutrality" in World War II) (1951).

5. Kolodkin, Pravovoi rezhim territorialnykh vod i otkrytogo moria (The Legal Regime of Territorial Waters and the High Seas) 11 (1961).

6. 3 Meshera, Morskoe pravo: pravovoi rezhim morskikh putei (Maritime Law; Legal Regime of Maritime Routes) 5 (1959).

7. Decree on the Protection of Fish and Furbearing Animals in the Northern Arctic Ocean and the White Sea, May 24, 1921, SU RSFSR (1921), no. 49, item 259; Decree on the Organization of the Administration of the Fishing Economy of the RSFSR, September 25, 1922, SU RSFSR (1922), no.61, item 780; Decree on the Procedure of Exploitation of the Fishing and Marine Furbearing Animal Trade in the Far East, March 2, 1923, SU RSFSR (1923), no. 36, item 378.

8. See Semyonov, Siberia: Its Conquest and Development (1963); Golder, Russian Expansion on the Pacific: 1641-1850 (1914).

9. Martens, *Sovremennoe mezhdunarodnoe pravo tsivilizovannykh narodov (Contemporary International Law of Civilized Peoples)* 383 (1898).

10. Zakharov, *Kurs obshchago mezhdunarodnogo prava (Course of General International Law)* 156-158 (1917).

11. Kamarovskii and Ulianitskii, *Mezhdunarodnoe pravo po lektsiiam (International Law Lectures)* 82-84 (1908).

12. Ulianitskii, *Mezhdunarodnoe pravo (International Law)* 87-89 (1911).

13. Kazanskii, *Uchebnik mezhdunarodnogo prava (Textbook on International Law)* 137-138 (1902).

14. Sivers, *Glavneishie svedeniia po morskomu mezhdunarodnomu pravu (The Most Important Information Concerning International Maritime Law)* 5 (1902); Stoianov, *Ocherki istorii i dogmatiki mezhdunarodnogo prava (Essays on the History and Dogmatics of International Law)* 356-363 (1875).

15. 13 Martens, *Sobranie traktatov i konventsii zakliuchennykh rossieiu s inostrannym derzhavami (Collection of Treaties and Conventions Concluded by Russia with Foreign Powers)* 201-234 (1875).

16. 4 Martens, *Recueil* 229-246.

17. 4 Martens, *Recueil* 315-336.

18. 22 *Polnoe sobranie zakonov rossisskoi imperii s 1649 goda (Complete Collection of the Laws of the Russian Empire Since 1649)* 968-972 (1830).

19. *Polnoe sobranie,* No. 28747.

20. Cited by Nikolaev, *Problema territorialnykh vod v mezhdunarodnom prave (Problem of Territorial Waters in International Law)* 57 (1954).

21. Fulton, *The Sovereignty of the Sea* 585 (1911).

22. Id.

23. 2 Smith, Great Britain and the Law of Nations 206 (1935).

24. Martens, op. cit. supra note 9, at 386-387.

25. Nikolaev, op. cit. supra note 20, at 58; Meyer, The Extent of Jurisdiction in Coastal Waters 237-238 (1937).

26. Meyer, Id.

27. The adoption of a new Customs Law in 1909, promulgated in 1910, provoked a large amount of unnecessary diplomatic correspondence. The law provided:

> To interpret in the following manner the fourth paragraph of the supplement to paragraph 2 of the Customs Regulations (Polnoe sobranie, Volume VI, 1904 ed.)
>
> 1. The surface of the water for twelve nautical miles from the extreme low-water mark from the seacoasts of the Russian Empire, whether mainland or islands, is recognized as the Marine Customs area, within the limits of which every vessel, whether Russian or foreign, is subject to supervision by those Russian authorities who are entrusted with guarding of the frontiers of the Empire.
>
> President of the Council of Empire
> December 10, 1909 M. Akimov

Great Britain and Japan protested vigorously; apparently under the impression that the twelve-mile limit had been adopted for all purposes. Their concern was heightened by the 1911 Russian decree establishing a twelve-mile fishing zone on the Far Eastern Coast. The United States Government entered no protest against either the Russian customs or fishing law. Its inquiries reflected a concern that the Russian Government might attempt to enforce the law against all vessels found within twelve miles of the shore, whether bound for a port or merely passing, without reference to whether such vessels were actually engaged in or suspected of being engaged upon a smuggling voyage. Indeed, no nation had ever protested against the customs laws of the United States or Great Britain which, in some cases, asserted jurisdiction over foreign vessels for the same distance as that provided for in the Russian customs law.

For an account of the discussion of the Russian customs and fishery laws from 1910-12, see Masterson, Jurisdiction in Marginal Seas 286 (1929).

28. This decree was the first to calculate the breadth of territorial waters from the lowest low water mark or "from the edge of the ice along the coast." 31 Polnoe sobranie 449-452 (3d ser.).

29. Note of the Russian Minister for Foreign Affairs to the Japanese Ambassador to Russia, (1912) Foreign Relations U.S. 1308 (1919).

30. Nikolaev, op. cit supra note 20, at 64.

31. SU RSFSR (1921), no. 49, item 259.

CHAPTER 2 SOVIET INTERNAL SEA WATERS

Internal waters are a constituent part of the coastal state and are subject to its complete sovereign authority. The navigation of foreign vessels may be totally prohibited in internal waters. All foreign vessels situated in internal waters, including warships, are obliged to observe local rules and customs. These principles are generally accepted by most international jurists. Soviet writers, however, have exhibited substantial differences of opinion as to which waters contiguous to the Soviet Union should be classified as internal.

The 1947 international law textbook represented the majority view of Soviet jurists up to that time when it defined "internal waters" as the waters of ports, as well as bays and gulfs whose shores belong to a single state and whose aperture does not exceed ten nautical miles. This definition was approved by the 1930 Hague Conference, and, in the Soviet view, had been accepted by the great majority of states.[1]

Since 1947, Soviet views have undergone important modifications. The 1951 international law textbook dropped the previous definition for one framed in terms of internal seas. These were seas fully encircled by the territory of a single state and seas whose shores are connected with another sea, both of which belong to the same state. Examples are the Sea of Azov and the White Sea,[2] where navigation and fishing by foreign vessels is prohibited by Soviet legislation.[3]

Bakhov partially restored the 1947 definition and acknowledged certain revisions in its application. He concluded that the waters of ports, roadsteads,[4] bays, gulfs, and estuaries whose shores belong to a single state, as well as some closed seas and border lakes, are internal waters, in addition to seas of the bay type which are encircled by the shores of a single state, though connected with the ocean by a strait or canal.[5]

Meshera subdivided Soviet internal waters into six Categories: (1) Soviet sea ports; (2) intrastate bays and seas which are under Soviet authority and whose aperture does not exceed twenty-four nautical miles; (3) historic bays and seas of the USSR as determined by special economic, defense, or other vital interests; (4) the Soviet part of the Caspian Sea; (5) water expanses along Soviet shores formed by tides; (6) water expanses between Soviet shores and straight baselines.[6]

Under the second Category, Meshera included the Sea of Azov, the White Sea, and the Riga Bay. The Kara, Laptev, and East Siberian Seas were subsumed within Category 3. Vereshchetin added the Chukotsk Sea to the third Category, and Shmigelskii mentioned the Aral Sea and Peter the Great Bay.[7]

The 1960 USSR statute on the state boundary defined "Soviet internal waters" as the waters of Soviet ports, the waters of bays, gulfs, inlets, and estuaries whose shore fully belongs to the USSR up to a straight line from shore to shore in a place where one or several apertures, each of which does not exceed twenty-four nautical miles in breadth, are formed leading into the sea, and the waters of bays, coves, inlets, and estuaries, seas and straits historically belonging to the Soviet Union.[8] The statute did not specify any historical bodies of water nor did it appear to encompass the latter three Categories posited by Meshera. Soviet writers do not regard the 1960 statute's list as being exhaustive, for maritime law textbooks published since 1960 include the waters between a straight base line and the shore as being part of the internal waters of the coastal state.[9] One might infer from the 1960 statute that the Soviet Union at present does not apply the straight base line principle to its coasts, although it acknowledged the validity of the principle in international law.

HISTORIC BAYS AND SEAS

Soviet jurists have long regarded historic bays and seas as part of the internal waters of a coastal state and subject to its unlimited sovereignty. In Soviet literature confusion has resulted from the classification of some bodies of water as both closed seas and historic bays. For example, in 1893 Russia claimed the White Sea as a closed sea, the 1956 naval international law manual described it as a historic bay,[10] and Meshera noted that it can be classified as a historic sea whose boundary is drawn from Sviatoi Nos to Kanin Nos and as an internal sea whose aperture does not exceed twenty-four nautical miles if the boundary is drawn from Cape Pogoredskii to the opposite shore near Cape Intsii.[11]

The number of bodies of water designated historic has been increasing. The 1947 international law textbook mentioned the White Sea, Sea of Azov, and Riga Bay as historic bays.[12] The 1951 international law textbook added "seas of the bay type"; i.e., the Kara, Laptev, East Siberian, and Chukotsk Seas.[13] Shmigelskii concurred in this classification,[14] but the 1956 naval international law manual treated historic bays and historic seas as separate entities.[15] The 1966 naval international law manual prefers the generic term "historic waters".[16] The ten-mile closing line rule was abandoned by the Soviet Union after the decision of the International Court of Justice in the Anglo-Norwegian Fisheries Case in 1951.

Historic bays and seas, though not designated by name, were expressly included within Soviet internal waters by the 1960 statute on the state boundary.[17] They are defined as having special economic or strategic significance for the littoral state or as having been established by historical tradition.[18] The criterion of special geographic conditions as an independent element has been added in the 1966 naval international law manual.[19] Although this formula has not been further elucidated, Soviet writers attempt to establish the presence of all factors in defending the designation of a body of water as historic. But the definition is stated in the alternative. Presumably the presence of any single factor could justify an application of the historic bay or sea principle in the Soviet view. However, it is going too far to say, as has one Western observer, that the "unilaterally proclaimed Soviet doctrine (of historic bays) virtually replaces the concept of the territorial sea belt."[20] The historic bay doctrine has been applied only to two bays and to the Arctic coastline, where arguments relating to historic, economic, and strategic factors find substantial support.

A celebrated recent application of the historic bay principle occurred on July 21, 1957, when the Council of Ministers of the USSR proclaimed Peter the Great Bay to be part of the internal waters of the Soviet Union.[21] The closing line established for the Bay was 108 miles in length. The Bay had never been previously mentioned by any Soviet writer as being an historic bay.[22]

Numerous diplomatic protests ensued, Japan being the most immediately aggrieved.[23] Soviet jurists defended the decree on historic grounds and on the basis that there was no generally accepted norm of international law with respect to the breadth of aperture of bays. They referred to Russian explorations during the 1850-60's, the founding of Vladivostok in 1860, and the enactment of fishing regulations in 1901 by the Tsarist Government in which "the fishing rights in the territorial waters of the Amur General-Governorship are granted only to Russian subjects . . ." with certain exceptions in the "southern part of the Primorye Region from the mouth of the Tiumen-Ula to Cape Povorotny."[24] A. N. Nikolaev denied a claim to a historic bay must be recognized by all states in order to be valid; this would be impossible and is not the general practice.[25] He noted Chinese support for the Soviet action as expressed in the Chinese press. Damage to Japanese fishing rights would be minimal since the Japanese in recent years had been largely excluded from the Bay. Although economic and strategic reasons were alluded to as justifying the decree, they were not elaborated.

Given the existence of historic, economic, and strategic factors, Romanov concluded that the 1957 decree merely synthesized previous legislation and established a boundary in the Bay wherein none had existed. The decree eliminated doubt with respect to the location of the Soviet boundary.[26]

The true reason for the unexpected Soviet "nationalization" of Peter the Great Bay remains ambiguous.

Perhaps there was concern that the impending Geneva Conference on the Law of the Sea in 1958 would adopt a binding rule on the length of the closing line for bays, thereby undermining the Soviet contention that a rule on the breadth of bays was not generally recognized in international law. A more probable explanation is that strategic considerations were paramount. Peter the Great Bay is the site of the port of Vladivostok, the major Soviet naval base in the Pacific theater and situated only ten miles from the Chinese frontier.

Soviet jurists compare the action of the Soviet Government with regard to Peter the Great Bay to the practice of other states: England (Bristol Bay); Canada (Hudson Bay, Bay of Fundy); and the United States (Chesapeake Bay).[27]

The historic bay doctrine was reasserted indirectly in March 1967 by the Soviet Government in an announcement that the Northern Sea Route would soon be opened to vessels of all foreign countries, with permission to refuel and use port facilities along the route. However, it is not clear that this policy differs from earlier practice. It may merely mean that the Soviet Union is undertaking to positively encourage, rather than tacitly permit, such voyages.[28]

NOTES

1. Durdenevskii and Krylov, Mezhdunarodnoe pravo (International Law) 246-247 (1947). We omit a discussion of inland rivers, lakes, and canals which are classified as internal or national waters.

2. Korovin, Mezhdunarodnoe pravo (International Law) 308 (1951).

3. Article 10, Ustav vnutrennogo vodnogo transporta SSSR (Charter of Internal Water Transport of the USSR). The Charter was adopted on October 15, 1955. No text or source has been located, although it was amended in 1958 and 1959. See Rechnoi transport v direktivakh kommunisticheskikh partii, zakonodatelnykh aktakh i

postanovlenii sovetskogo pravitelstva (1918-1959) (River Transport in Directives of the Communist Party, and Legislative Acts and Decrees of the Soviet Government (1918-1959)) 195-196 (1959).

Article 13 of the Decree on the Regulation of Fishing and the Protection of Fish Reserves, September 25, 1935, SZ SSSR (1935), no. 50, item 420.

4. Bakhov, Voenno-morskoi mezhdunarodno-pravovoi spravochnik (Naval International Law Manual) 113 (1956). Keilin and Zhudro concur with this view, but Vereshchetin considers roadsteads to be part of territorial waters, as do the 1947 and 1951 international law textbooks.

5. Bakhov, ibid., at 114.

6. Meshera, Morskoe pravo: pravovoi rezhim morskikh putei (Maritime Law; Legal Regime of Maritime Routes) 10 (1959).

7. Vereshchetin, Svoboda sudokhodstva v otkrytom more (Freedom of Navigation on the High Seas) 7 (1958); Shmigelskii and Iasinovskii, Osnovy sovetskogo morskogo prava (Fundamental Principles of Soviet Maritime Law) 29 (1959).

8. Article 4, Statute on Protection of the State Boundary of the USSR, August 5, 1960, Vedomosti SSSR (1960), No. 34, item 324.

9. Zhudro, et. al., Morskoe pravo (Maritime Law) 98-99 (1964).

10. Bakhov, op. cit. supra note 4, at 114-115.

11. Meshera, op. cit. supra note 6, at 10.

12. Durdenevskii and Krylov, op. cit. supra note 1, at 248. The 1966 naval international law manual cites a note of the RSFSR to Norway of May 4, 1922, as confirming the status of the White Sea as a historic body of water. The note is translated in the documentary appendix.

13. Korovin, op. cit. supra note 2, at 296.

14. Shmigelskii, op. cit. supra note 7, at 35.

15. Bakhov, op. cit. supra note 4, at 118, 119.

16. Barabolia, et. al., Voenno-morskoi mezhdunarodno-pravovoi spravochnik (Naval International Law Manual) 215 (1966).

17. Article 4, 1960 statute, op. cit. supra note 8.

18. Kozhevnikov, International Law 205-206 (1961); Zhudro, op. cit. supra note 9, at 98. Kozhevnikov's volume was published in Russian in 1957 and partially updated in the English translation.

19. Barabolia, op. cit. supra note 16, at 216.

20. Harben, "Soviet Attitudes and Practices Concerning Maritime Waters: A Recent Historical Survey," 15 JAG Journal 149-154, 160 (1961). Harben writes that the Soviet coastline is bounded by historic bays and seas. He confuses the closed or regional sea with the historic bay. But Soviet jurists have begun to suggest that the Okhotsk Sea is an internal Russian sea by virtue of an Instruction of the Tsarist Government of 1853 concerning protection of Okhotsk shores. See Kozhevnikov, Kurs mezhdunarodnogo prava (Textbook of International Law) 213-214 (2d ed. 1966).

21. Izvestia, July 21, 1957, p. 1; An approximate English translation is given by Strohl, The International Law of Bays 350 (1963).

22. Bouchez, The Regime of Bays in International Law 225 (1964). See Strohl, ibid., at 332-367 for an extensive discussion of Peter the Great Bay.

23. Bouchez, ibid. Diplomatic protests were presented by: The Netherlands (October 31, 1957); Japan (July 26, 1957 and January 17, 1958); United States (August 12, 1957 and August 6, 1958); United Kingdom (September 10, 1957);

France (October 11, 1957); Sweden (December 9, 1957); Federal Republic of Germany (February 5, 1958).

24. Nikolaev, "O zalive Petra Velikogo," (On Peter the Great Bay) 1958 Mezhdunarodnaia zhizn (International Affairs), no. 2, pp. 50-57.

25. Recognition on the part of other states of one or another bay as a "historic bay" belonging to the littoral state does not have, from the viewpoint of international law, decisive significance.

See Barabolia, op. cit. supra note 16, at 216.

26. Romanov, "Zaliv Petra Velikogo -- vnutrennie vody sovetskogo soiuza," (Peter the Great Bay -- Internal Waters of the Soviet Union) 1958 Sovetskoe gosudarstvo i pravo (Soviet State and Law), no. 5, p. 53.

27. Barabolia, op. cit. supra note 16, at 217.

28. The New York Times, March 29, 1967, p. 1. Soviet publicists contend that the Anglo-Norwegian Fisheries decision of the International Court of Justice supports the extension of the regime of internal waters to water routes developed by the coastal state. See Kozhevnikov, Kurs mezhdunarodnogo prava (Textbook of International Law) 213 (2d ed. 1966).

CHAPTER 3 CLOSED SEAS

The closed sea concept was revived by Soviet jurists in the early post-World War II period in order to terminate or to severely restrict the access of vessels of hostile or potentially hostile powers to the Black Sea. The concept is controversial and has been applied inconsistently in Soviet maritime literature.

Prior to World War II, the closed sea was rarely mentioned in Soviet works on maritime or international law. Some jurists regarded the White Sea as a closed sea, citing the opinions of F. F. Martens and other prerevolutionary writers. The most common approach was that adopted in the 1947 international law textbook, which regarded the Caspian Sea and Aral Sea as closed, although acknowledging that these bodies of water were more analogous to large lakes.[1]

In 1948 B. A. Dranov published his classic work on the Black Sea Straits. On the basis of eighteenth and nineteenth century Russian-Turkish treaties, Dranov argued that the Black Sea was a closed sea whose regime should be established by the coastal states. The closed character of the Black Sea was affected, in addition, by the juridical nature of the Straits. Dranov distinguished among three categories of straits: (1) those leading into internal seas (the shores of which belong to one state); (2) those leading into a closed sea; (3) those connecting with the high seas and oceans. The regime of the second category must be regulated by those states most interested in the freedom of commercial shipping and security of the sea; i.e., the coastal states.[2] S. V. Molodtsov applied Dranov's thesis to the Baltic Sea.[3] Both views were incorporated in a more systematic fashion into the 1951 international law textbook, which referred to the Caspian, Black, and Baltic Seas as closed, despite minor differences in regime. In the case of the latter two seas, only the coastal states enjoy freedom of navigation and maritime business. Commercial navigation by noncoastal states may be permitted in the interests of international trade.[4]

Keilin accepted this definition in his work on maritime law.[5] Other jurists refined and expanded the doctrine. Bakhov and others differentiated among three types of closed sea: (1) a sea fully enclosed by the territory of two or several states which has no entrance to another sea; i.e., the Caspian; (2) a sea enclosed by a limited number of states which is connected with other seas by one or several narrow straits whose regime is regulated by an international convention; i.e., the Black and Baltic Seas; (3) a sea enclosed by the territory of two or several states which is not regulated by international convention; i.e., the Sea of Japan and the Okhotsk Sea. Each category must also be characterized by the fact that no basic maritime routes of international significance pass through the sea.[6]

> States not contiguous to these seas can not and do not have any legal grounds for claiming participation in deciding questions concerning the regime of navigation in closed seas or in the straits leading to these seas.[7]

However, the merchant vessels of noncontiguous states are said to have equal rights with those of coastal states. During peacetime, the regime for merchant vessels in a closed sea is the same as the high seas, except for straits regulations. The warships of contiguous states enjoy a right of free and unlimited navigation in closed seas outside the territorial waters of other contiguous states. Warships of noncontiguous states have no right of access to closed seas.

Shmigelskii, who listed the Black Sea, Baltic Sea, Okhotsk Sea, and the Sea of Japan as being closed, noted that the regime of the latter three seas "is subject to establishment."[8] Siling evidently would permit the prohibition of commercial navigation by noncontiguous states in a closed sea.[9]

Recently, some Soviet jurists have been disturbed by the inconsistent and incorrect applications of the closed sea doctrine by their colleagues. Vereshchetin has pointed out that in Western literature the term "closed sea" is frequently used as the antonym of "high seas"; that is, it is applied to all expanses of sea to which the regime of the high seas does not extend.[10] To prerevolutionary Russian and Western jurists the closed sea was closed to vessels of noncontiguous states for all purposes.

Another jurist, S. A. Malinin, has urged the term "regional sea" to replace "closed sea" in Soviet literature. Malinin defined regional seas as expanses of water enclosed by the territory of two or several states which are connected with the high seas by a strait or canal and which are significant as a maritime route only to the contiguous states. There are four independent legal requirements for a closed or regional sea: (1) a particular geographic configuration of the shore; (2) the proximity of the shore to a limited number of states whose territory fully encloses the given expanse of water; (3) limited possibilities of access to the sea (comparatively narrow entrances); (4) absence of international maritime routes.

From these premises Malinin concluded the regime of the closed or regional sea required the consideration of the vital interests, primarily security, of the coastal states and the establishment of a regime within the exclusive competence of the coastal states. The specific norms of the regime would depend upon an agreement by the contiguous states. However, military maneuvers and navigation by warships of noncontiguous powers may be prohibited, but commercial navigation by noncontiguous merchant vessels may not.[11]

In accordance with Malinin's analysis, the Aral Sea is a lake rather than a closed sea because it has no direct or indirect connections with oceans. Malinin contended that the Caspian Sea, regarded as a closed sea by Vereshchetin,[12] Bakhov,[13] and others, is also a lake because navigation of merchant vessels of noncontiguous states is prohibited and because international law norms do not apply to the Caspian.

Vereshchetin concurred that security interests of contiguous states are the primary factor in determining the closed or regional status of a body of water.[14] They stressed, in an effort to make the closed sea doctrine more palatable, that merchant vessels of noncontiguous states cannot be excluded under international law from the closed sea. This principle is the major distinction between the closed "lake" and the closed or regional sea.

The 1966 naval international law manual accepted the differentiations among three types of closed sea contained in the 1956 edition. More emphasis, however, was placed on historical and legal precedents affecting the regime of closed seas in comparison with the predominantly geographic orientation of the earlier publications.

Closed seas, the authors maintained, in diplomatic and treaty practice are those which for historical reasons or pursuant to international agreements a special regime has been established closing the sea or restricting the navigation of warships and military aircraft of noncontiguous states. Water expanses of closed seas beyond the territorial waters of the coastal states are available for the common enjoyment of all littoral states on the basis of equality and a just appraisal of their interests. One coastal state may not disregard the economic and security interests of another littoral state. The manual authors concurred with the majority of Soviet jurists that closed seas are open in peacetime to the commercial shipping of all countries of the world.[15] But the reference to the exclusion of military aircraft of noncontiguous states had not been made in previous works.

Although the 1958 Geneva Conference on the Law of the Sea declined to discuss the principle of closed seas, Soviet jurists insist that generally recognized principles of international law, treaties and conventions, and historical precedents provide sufficient basis for determining the legal status of closed seas. With respect to the Black and Baltic Seas, "the littoral states have long considered the seas closed to warships of nonlittoral states."[16] Turko-Russian treaties of 1793, 1805, and 1833 are cited to support Russian claims to the Black Sea.[17] For the Soviet period, the authors cite a note of the RSFSR to Great Britain demanding the removal from the Black and Baltic Seas of "warships of all those nations which do not have possessions on their shores."[18] The Soviet Union refused to ratify the 1923 Lausanne Convention, which opened the Black Sea to warships of all states, but did ratify the 1936 Montreux Convention limiting the access of warships of noncontiguous states.

The argument relating to the Baltic and other seas is comparable, but even less tenable. Soviet jurists cite treaties between Denmark and Sweden (February 26, 1658); Russia and Sweden (March 9, 1759); the League of Armed Neutrality Conventions of 1780-1781; and a convention between Russia, Denmark, Sweden, and Prussia (December 16, 1800) to support the proposition that the Baltic has been closed from "time immemorial". Unspecified provisions of the 1920 peace treaty between Finland and the RSFSR and a proposal of the Soviet Government at the 1924 Conference on the Limitation of Naval Armaments to close the Baltic are the sole materials from the twentieth century. The "closed" regime of the Sea of Japan and the Okhotsk Sea has no historical or legal precedent. Not traversed by sea or ocean routes of international significance, and bordered only by the Soviet Union, Japan, North Korea, and South Korea, these two seas have been the subject of repeated Soviet proposals to exclude warships and military aircraft of noncontiguous states from their waters. These proposals, as the 1966 naval international law manual conceded, "have not been accepted."[19] The Caspian Sea, landlocked and governed by bilateral treaties and national legislation, is a unique case. Few would disagree with considering it the prototype of the closed sea recognized by international law.

The closed sea doctrine in its Soviet formulation is an attempt to lay the basis for excluding the Western powers from the Western and Eastern sea approaches to Soviet territory and from participating in the creation or modification of any special regime affecting these approaches. The doctrine has found little favor in international law, nor is it likely to do so unless the Soviet Union becomes overwhelmingly preponderant, politically and militarily, in the Pacific, Baltic, and Near East regions. Historical and legal precedents cited by Soviet writers are inaccurate, obsolete, or clearly overruled by subsequent developments.

Thus, the 1920 note from the RSFSR to Great Britain protested an order given by the British Government authorizing British vessels to attack Russian submarines in the Black and Baltic Seas without warning. The full text of the paragraph partially quoted reads:

> The Soviet Government would consider withdrawal from these waters of warships of all those nations which have no possessions on their shores as the best means of preventing any armed skirmishes both in the Black and in the Baltic Seas.[20]

The note did not refer to the closed sea doctrine nor make any claim relating to exclusive jurisdiction of the littoral states over these waters, nor assert the illegality of British presence in the area.

Soviet jurists have refrained from applying the closed sea doctrine to bodies of water not contiguous to the Soviet Union and from passing judgment on the claims made by other states to closed seas. Events in 1967 involving the Gulf of Aqaba, which Arab jurists have claimed is a closed body of water, testify to the explosive and disruptive potential of the closed sea theory, if applied generally. One is inclined to agree with Hartingh's observation: "It is incontestable that this theory of 'closed seas' constitutes a menacing danger to the freedom of the seas."[21]

NOTES

1. Durdenevskii and Krylov, Mezhdunarodnoe pravo (International Law) 237 (1947). Contrary to the assertion of a Western authority on Soviet law, the Soviet closed sea doctrine is not an extension of mare clausum. See Grzybowski, "The Soviet Doctrine of Mare Clausum and Policies in Black and Baltic Seas," 14 Journal of Central European Affairs 339-353 (1955).

2. Dranov, Chernomorskie provliy: mezhdunarodno-pravovoi rezhim (The Black Sea Straits: International Legal Regime) 227 (1948).

3. Molodtsov, Mezhdunarodno-pravovoi rezhim baltiiskikh prolivov (International Legal Regime of the Baltic Straits) (1950).

4. Durdenevskii and Krylov, op. cit. supra note 1, at 309.

5. Keilin, Sovetskoe morskoe pravo (Soviet Maritime Law) 61 (1954).

6. Bakhov, Voenno-morskoi mezhdunarodno-pravovoi spravochnik (Naval International Law Manual) 53 (1956).

7. Ibid. at 54.

8. Shmigelskii and Iasinovskii, Osnovy sovetskogo morskogo prava (Fundamental Principles of Soviet Maritime Law) 35 (1963).

9. Siling, Morskoe pravo (Maritime Law) 64 (1964).

10. Vereshchetin, Svoboda sudokhodstva v otkrytom more (Freedom of Navigation on the High Seas) 11 (1958).

11. Malinin, "K voprosu o pravovoi klassifikatsii vodnykh prostranstv," (On the Question of the Legal Classification of Water Expanses) 46 Informatsionnyi sbornik. Morskoe pravo i praktika (Information Handbook. Maritime Law and Practice) 13-19 (1960).

12. Vereshchetin, op. cit. supra note 10, at 8.

13. Bakhov, op. cit. supra note 6, at 53, 256. Siling uses the designation "regional seas" in his recent work but erroneously places the Caspian Sea in the category of being open to merchant vessels of all nations. See Siling, op. cit. supra note 9, at 63.

14. Vereshchetin, op. cit. supra note 10, at 11.

15. Barabolia, et. al., Voenno-morskoi mezhdunarodno-pravovoi spravochnik (Naval International Law Manual) 129 (1966).

16. Ibid. at 130.

17. Ibid. For a highly critical analysis of Russian and Soviet scholarship relating to these treaties, see Hurewitz, "Russia and the Turkish Straits: A Reevaluation of the Origins of the Problem," 14 World Politics 605-632 (1962).

18. Barabolia, ibid. at 131.

19. Id. at 133.

20. Note of the RSFSR to Great Britain of October 19, 1920, 3 Dokumenty 285-287.

21. Hartingh, Les Conceptions Sovietiques du Droit de la Mer 30 (1960).

CHAPTER 4 SOVIET TERRITORIAL WATERS

TERMINOLOGY

In 1960 a Soviet legal scholar commented that there is no firmly established legal classification of water expanses along Soviet coasts.[1] Soviet legislation has employed a variety of terms in referring to waters bordering Soviet shores. These include: "coastal waters" (pribrezhnye vody); "coastal belt of waters" (pribrezhnaia polosa vod); "territorial belt of waters"; "sea border belt" (morskaia pogranichnaia polosa); "sea belt"; "shore waters" (beregovye vody). "Territorial waters" has been preferred by Soviet legislators. The term was used in eight of twenty-two normative acts directly relating to questions of Soviet territorial waters and in thirty-five treaties concluded by the RSFSR, the Ukraine, and the USSR with other nations up to 1954. The term was not used, however, in the majority of normative acts (14 of 22); in particular, it was not employed in the 1927 statute on the state boundary, which is commonly cited as having codified the Soviet twelve-mile rule. Nevertheless, A. N. Nikolaev urged in 1954 that Soviet jurists ought to unite in using "territorial waters" because it was the term predominantly found in Soviet international treaty practice and diplomatic correspondence and "doubtless . . . will be used in our further legislation relating to territorial waters." He assailed those Soviet jurists "who attempt to defend the term 'territorial sea', which has not existed and does not exist in Soviet practice and which does not predominate in international practice."[2]

Most Soviet writers adopted the term,[3] and it was incorporated into Article 3 of the 1960 statute on the state boundary. The 1956 naval international law manual preferred "territorial waters" because "it more correctly reflects the nature of the waters designated and . . . the connection of the sea belt with the territory and the 'internal sea waters' of the coastal state."[4] But Vereshchetin has argued that the 1958 Geneva Convention on the Territorial Sea adopted the term "territorialnoe more." He can find nothing in Soviet practice or legislation which obliges Soviet writers to refrain from using that term. The 1966 naval international law manual has retained the term "territorial waters".[5]

This was not idle bickering over semantic nuances. Some Soviet jurists had denied the existence of a twelve-mile belt of territorial waters, pointing to the discrepancies in Soviet legislative terminology. Some jurists also regarded territorial waters as a part of the high seas over which the littoral state had certain limited rights. These writers preferred terminology which stressed the relationship of territorial water belts to the high seas rather than to the coastal state.

DEFINITION

Several Soviet jurists have contended that the Soviet Union had no territorial waters fully subordinate to its sovereignty, but that the Soviet Union had special zones in which it exercised special rights. The staunchest advocate of this position was V. A. Belli, compiler of the official naval international law manual in 1939.[6] Belli regarded territorial waters as part of the high seas subject to certain rights of the coastal state. He noted that "legislation of the USSR does not define the breadth of territorial waters of the Soviet Union . . .", but ". . . establishes border and customs zones, fishing zones, zones for the use of wireless radio equipment, fortified zones, and zones closed to navigation."[7]

Nikolaev pronounced such views not only mistaken, but harmful, for "they weaken our position in the struggle for the exercise of the sovereign rights of the USSR in its territorial waters, they help our adversaries in their struggle against us, and in their attempts to violate the regime of our Soviet territorial waters."[8] He defined Soviet territorial waters as a "constituent part of the territory of the USSR, under its sovereignty and its state ownership."[9] This definition, in his opinion, was affirmed in the following Soviet legislation: (1) Article 6 of the Constitution of the USSR which declared that waters are part of state ownership; (2) the 1927 statute on the state boundary which established a twelve-mile belt of waters; (3) the 1935 Air Code of the USSR which placed air space above territorial waters under exclusive Soviet sovereignty; (4) the 1935 decree on fishing which transformed territorial waters into a maritime fishery reserve of the USSR. In addition, Nikolaev maintained that the Soviet Union assumed by right of state succession the twelve-mile limit established by the Tsarist Government.[10]

The difficulties of Nikolaev's position were manifold. The Constitution of the USSR does not specify territorial waters; the 1927 statute did not use the term territorial waters; the 1935 Air Code did not delimit territorial waters; the 1935 decree referred only to fishing rights; and the Tsarist Government had effectively established only a twelve-mile customs zone and a fishing zone on the Pacific coast. Soviet legislation governing territorial waters was confusing and contradictory. Even in attempting to enforce a twelve-mile limit in the Baltic Sea against Scandinavian fishing vessels, the Soviet Government had to be pressed before it finally revealed its claim to jurisdiction was founded on the 1927 statute on the state boundary.[11] Not until adoption of the 1960 statute on the state boundary did the twelve-mile limit of territorial waters find unequivocal support in Soviet legislation.

Belli and Nikolaev represented extreme points on the spectrum of Soviet concepts of territorial waters. Pashukanis stated that territorial waters were subject to a special regime in accordance with the security, military, sanitary, and fiscal interests of the coastal state. Although he recognized that there are two points of view about whether territorial waters are an integral portion of the littoral state, he did not take a position himself. However, he did treat the twelve-mile limit on fishing as strictly a fishing regulation without reference to the 1927 statute on the state boundary.[12]

Authorities in the postwar era have preferred Nikolaev's definition. The 1947 and 1951 international law textbooks affirmed the sovereignty of the coastal state, but differed from Nikolaev in asserting that the coastal state may not limit the right of innocent passage. The 1956 naval international law manual defined territorial waters as a belt of a definite breadth extending along the coast which is a constituent part of the territory of the coastal state and subject to its sovereignty. This definition was said to accord with the practice of the majority of states.[13] Kolodkin accepted this definition with the addition of an important clause, "taking into account generally recognized norms of international law."[14]

Under the provisions of the 1958 Geneva Convention on the Territorial Sea and the 1960 statute on the state boundary, the current Soviet view has been aptly summarized by Koretskii:

> The sovereignty of a coastal state in the territorial sea serves as the basis of the rights of that state with respect to passing foreign vessels. Recognition of the sovereignty of a coastal state signifies recognition of those rights which that state exercises in its territorial sea. By virtue of the existence of the sovereignty of a coastal state in its territorial sea, the state has the exclusive right to publish acts concerning the regulation of the regime in these waters -- security, sanitary, business, navigation, and resources. The totality of norms defining the rights and duties of a coastal state and passing vessels is the legal regime of the territorial sea.[15]

BREADTH OF TERRITORIAL WATERS

The Soviet Government adhered to the position of the Tsarist Government that there was no generally recognized breadth of territorial waters in international law.[16] Soviet members of the International Law Commission and delegates to the Geneva Conference on the Law of the Sea repeatedly declared that the Soviet Union "applied the twelve-mile limit; that breadth had been determined by Russia half a century ago."[17]

Soviet normative acts adopted different limits for different purposes. The fishing decree of 1921 established a twelve-mile fishing zone in Arctic waters and the White Sea;[18] an instruction of July 5, 1924, regulating the navigation of vessels in coastal waters within zones of firing from shore batteries in peacetime seemed to apply the cannon shot rule;[19] a decree of July 24, 1928, set forth a ten-mile zone regulating the use of wireless radio equipment;[20] the 1927 statute on the state boundary established a twelve-mile limit but did not specify that a belt of territorial waters had been delimited.[21]

The 1960 statute on the state boundary codified the twelve-mile limit as the breadth of Soviet territorial waters unless provided otherwise by agreements of the USSR with other states. There are several exceptions. Under the 1940 peace treaty with Finland, a three-mile limit was established at the northern extremity of Sursari Island in order to secure freedom of passage for vessels sailing to the north.[22] A Soviet-Finnish agreement concluded May 20, 1965, established a breadth of territorial waters less than twelve miles in the Gulf of Finland.[23] In the straits between the Japanese Island of Hokkaido and the Soviet Kurile Islands, and in the Bering Strait, a median line currently forms the boundary.[24]

MANNER OF CALCULATING THE BREADTH OF USSR TERRITORIAL WATERS

The breadth of Soviet territorial waters is calculated from the normal base line both on the mainland and around islands or from the extreme point of the internal sea waters of the Soviet Union.[25] Because of the special configuration of the shores and an insignificant difference in the ebb and flow of the tides, the breadth of Soviet territorial waters in the Gulf of Finland (where there are reefs) has been calculated from the farthest islands or rocks protruding above the surface of the water. This method was originally established in Article 3 of the 1920 peace treaty between Finland and the RSFSR. Although the treaty was no longer in force, Nikolaev believed that practical expediency has preserved this method of measuring Soviet territorial waters in the Gulf of Finland.[26] Nikolaev also approved the principle of calculating the breadth of territorial waters from the edge of stationary ice attached to the shore.[27] Soviet jurists recognize the straight base line method as set forth in the 1958 Geneva Convention on the Territorial Sea, although prior to its adoption Uustal rejected the notion of a maximum length of a base line and a maximum distance from shore to the base line.[28] However, there has been no reference to the base line method being applied to Soviet coasts.

The outward line of territorial waters is the state boundary of the Soviet Union at sea. In areas where Soviet territorial waters adjoin the territorial waters of a neighboring state, the maritime lateral state boundary is established in accordance with agreements concluded with these states. Examples of such agreements include that of February 15, 1957, between the Soviet Union and Norway and a Protocol of March 18, 1958, between the Soviet Union and Poland. In the absence of an agreement, the state boundary is determined in accordance with the principles of international practice of states or is the straight line extending the land boundary seaward.[29]

NOTES

1. Malinin, "K voprosu o pravovoi klassifikatsii vodnykh prostranstv," (On the Question of the Legal Classification of Water Expanses) 46 Informatsionnyi sbornik. Morskoe pravo i praktika (Information Handbook. Maritime Law and Practice) 13 (1960).

2. Nikolaev, Problema territorialnykh vod v mezhdunarodnom prave (Problem of Territorial Waters in International Law) 199-200 (1954).

3. Keilin, Nikolaev, and Uustal, among others, prefer this term.

4. Bakhov, Voenno-morskoi mezhdunarodno-pravovoi spravochnik (Naval International Law Manual) 56 (1956).

5. Barabolia, et. al., Voenno-morskoi mezhdunarodno-pravovoi spravochnik (Naval International Law Manual) (1966).

6. Belli, Voenno-morskoi mezhdunarodno-pravovoi spravochnik (Naval International Law Manual) (2 vols. 1939-1940). Copies of this work, which contains the texts of many otherwise unobtainable decrees and instructions regulating maritime matters, are apparently not available in the libraries of the United States, Canada, or France.

7. Ibid. at 10-13, as cited by Nikolaev, op. cit. supra note 2, at 202-203. Belli's view was supported by Keilin and Vinogradov, Morskoe pravo (Maritime Law) (1939).

8. Nikolaev, ibid., at 203.

9. Id. at 204.

10. Id.

11. Schapiro, "The Limits of Russian Territorial Waters in the Baltic," 27 British Yearbook of International Law 440 (1950).

12. Pashukanis, Ocherki po mezhdunarodnomu pravu (Outlines of International Law) 120-121 (1935).

13. Bakhov, op. cit. supra note 4, at 81.

14. Kolodkin, Pravovoi rezhim territorialnykh vod i otkrytogo moria (The Legal Regime of Territorial Waters and the High Seas) 7 (1961).

15. Koretskii and Tunkin, Ocherki mezhdunarodnogo morskogo prava (Outlines of International Maritime Law) 54 (1962).

16. See Note of the Government of the RSFSR to the Government of Great Britain, May 7, 1923. 6 Dokumenty 279-284. This position was the basis of Soviet proposals

that the Geneva Conferences on the Law of the Sea adopt a twelve-mile limit for territorial waters:

> In the past, the crucial issue of the breadth of the territorial sea had been determined by each coastal state in accordance with geographical considerations, so that different limits had been fixed . . . Tunkin, 3 U.N. Conf. on Law of the Sea 31 (1958).

17. Tunkin, ibid. at 31. Also see Koretskii's Statement to the Second U.N. Conf. on the Law of the Sea: Official Records at 116 (1960) (A/CONF.19/8); Krylov, in (1955), 1 Yb. Int'l L. Comm. 156 (1956).

18. SU RSFSR (1921), no. 49, item 259.

19. Cited by Nikolaev, op, cit. supra note 2, at 200.

20. SZ SSSR (1929), no. 48, item 431.

21. SZ SSSR (1927), no. 62, item 625.

22. 10 SDD 11-17.

23. Barabolia, op. cit. supra note 5, at 47.

24. Id.

25. Article 3, Statute on Protection of the State Boundary of the USSR, August 5, 1960, Vedomosti SSSR (1960), no. 34, item 324.

26. Nikolaev, op. cit. supra note 2, at 207.

27. Id.

28. Uustal, "Osnovnye voprosy pravovogo rezhima territorialnykh vod," (Fundamental Questions of the Legal Regime of Territorial Waters) 1957 Sovetskoe gosudarstvo i pravo, no. 6, p. 75.

29. Barabolia, op. cit. supra note 5, at 48.

CHAPTER 5 INNOCENT PASSAGE

The Soviet Union initially was opposed to prevailing conceptions of international law for both ideological and practical reasons. Ideologically, the several schools of international legal thought were not considered compatible with Marxist theories of man and state; practically, it was believed that the acceptance of existing international law norms would impose restraints derived from customs which the Soviet Union had no part in forming or from treaties concluded by a bourgeois regime whose national interests and social philosophy were totally alien to those of the dictatorship of the proletariat.[1]

SOVIET LEGISLATION REGULATING INNOCENT PASSAGE

The regime of navigation in Soviet territorial waters was influenced foremost by the need to protect the Russian coast from incursions of hostile naval vessels and by the interest in developing Soviet foreign trade. The Finnish-RSFSR peace treaty secured the right for passenger and merchant vessels belonging to Russia to use all channels open to Finnish vessels in the latter's territorial waters, conditional upon the observance of provisions concerning the pilotage of foreign vessels.[2] Other peace treaties forbade, "except in cases provided for in international law," the launching, passage, or navigation of any warships belonging either to organizations or groups whose object was to make war or to countries which were in a state of war with either of the contracting parties.[3] Commercial treaties concluded in 1924-1927 with Italy, Sweden, Germany, Norway, Turkey, and other states contained provisions, conditional on reciprocity, affecting the passage, rights, and duties of vessels belonging to the contracting parties.[4]

The New Economic Policy of the 1920's brought about a measure of stability and opportunity for the consolidation of internal authority. The Soviet Government began to codify and extend its authority over the passage of foreign vessels in its territorial waters. In 1921 a Decree on the Protection of Fisheries and Furbearing Animals in the Arctic Ocean and the White Sea prohibited foreign vessels from fishing in the White Sea or within a twelve-mile fishing zone in the northern Arctic ocean.[5] The use of wireless radio equipment by foreign vessels in Soviet territorial waters was restricted by a 1923 decree, as was the exploitation of fishing and aquatic furbearing animals in the Far East.[6]

The sole normative act to expressly mention innocent passage (mirnyi prokhod; literally, "peaceful passage") until 1960 was an instruction of July 5, 1924, regulating the navigation of vessels in territorial waters within zones of firing from shore batteries in peacetime. It provided: "Merchant vessels of the USSR and merchant vessels of foreign states shall have the right of unhindered navigation within territorial waters, except for special zones."[7]

The 1927 statute on the state boundary did not mention the right of innocent passage.[8] It did, however, significantly broaden the scope of Soviet authority over the innocent passage of foreign vessels. All nonmilitary vessels without distinction of flag became subject to control by the border guard of the Unified State Political Administration (OGPU) (Art. 23). Within a twelve-mile maritime belt all nonmilitary vessels could be stopped and searched by the border guard; masters of vessels subject to search were obliged to present all documents in their possession relating to the vessel and cargo (Art. 25). Nonmilitary vessels could be arrested (a) if the master did not present all relevant documents relating to vessel and cargo; (b) if the vessel loaded or unloaded cargo or embarked or disembarked persons in territorial waters without proper authorization; or (c) if the vessel engaged in hunting or fishing or any other maritime trade in a prohibited area, or in a free area without proper authorization (Art. 26).

In 1960, as part of sweeping revisions in several areas of Soviet legislation and in response to the 1958 Geneva

Convention on the Territorial Sea, the Soviet Union adopted a new Statute on the Protection of the State Boundary of the USSR and announced new regulations governing the passage of foreign warships through Soviet territorial waters.

With respect to innocent passage, the provisions of the 1960 statute may be summarized as follows:

(a) Foreign nonmilitary vessels enjoy a right of innocent passage through the territorial waters of the USSR. Passage is defined as navigation through territorial waters for the purpose of traversing them without entering internal waters or of proceeding to internal waters or of departing from internal waters for the high seas. Passage is considered innocent if a vessel follows a customary navigational course or a course recommended by competent agencies while observing the established regime of territorial waters, and in areas not closed to navigation. (Art. 15)

(b) Foreign warships are to pass through territorial waters and enter internal waters of the USSR in accordance with the previous authorization of the USSR Government in the manner provided for by Special Rules for the visits of foreign warships. Foreign submarines permitted entrance to Soviet territorial and internal waters must navigate on the surface. (Art. 16)

(c) Foreign warships and nonmilitary vessels, while present in Soviet territorial waters, must observe radio, port, customs, sanitary, and other rules established for navigation. (Art. 17)

(d) Nonobservance by nonmilitary vessels of the rules for innocent passage because of damage or entry in distress must be immediately communicated to the authorities of the nearest Soviet port. Sending a false signal for the purpose of illegal entry into USSR territorial waters or arrival in those waters is considered to be a violation of the USSR state boundary, and the offending ship is subject to detention. (Art. 18)

(e) The conduct of maritime trade (fishing, crabbing, hunting, etc.) by foreign vessels is prohibited in USSR territorial waters except as provided for by agreements with other states. Foreign vessels are also prohibited from conducting hydrographic work and research in these waters. Violation entails detention of the vessel and the bringing of persons to responsibility under the criminal codes of the union republics. (Art. 19)

(f) For the purposes of the statute, violators of the state boundary of the USSR include foreign warships and nonmilitary vessels in territorial waters which violate the established rules of entrance. (Art. 26)

(g) With respect to foreign nonmilitary vessels, the Soviet border guard has the right: (1) to request a vessel to show its national flag if it is not raised and to inquire as to the purposes of entrance into Soviet territorial waters; (2) to request a vessel to change course if it is in an area temporarily or permanently closed; (3) to stop a vessel and conduct an inspection when the vessel is in a closed area, is moving outside established channels or a recommended course, lies adrift, anchors, does not reply to signals for an inspection or for a change in course, or when a vessel violates rules established by the statute. An inspection includes verification of the shipping and navigational documents, documents of the officers and crew, passengers, and cargo, and in necessary instances, of the ship's quarters; (4) to take from the vessel and to detain persons who have committed crimes and who are subject to criminal responsibility under USSR and union republic legislation and to transfer them to the appropriate agencies. These measures may not be applied to a person on board a foreign vessel traversing Soviet territorial waters who has committed a crime prior to the entrance of the vessel in the territorial waters if the ship is proceeding from a foreign port, restricts its passage to territorial waters, and does not enter internal waters; (5) to pursue and detain ship-violators of the Soviet state boundary. (Art. 36) Article 36 does not apply to foreign warships.

(h) Any foreign nonmilitary vessels in USSR territorial waters may be detained by the border guard and brought to the nearest port: (1) for violation of zones permanently or temporarily closed; (2) for loading or unloading cargo or persons in unauthorized places without the permission of competent agencies; (3) for conducting maritime trade or hydrographic work and research in USSR territorial waters; (4) for intentionally damaging navigational markers, cables, and other submerged or protruding objects belonging to the USSR; (5) when the vessel's master does not present shipping and cargo documents; (6) for refusal of the vessel to obey instructions of USSR authorities; (7) in all other instances of violation of rules established in the statute. (Art. 37)

For every instance of inspection or detention of a vessel, an official document must be drawn up and signed by the commander of the border guard vessel and the master of the inspected or detained vessel. If the captain of the inspected or detained vessel considers the actions of the border guard vessel or other vessel's master to be incorrect or does not agree with the contents of the document, he may make a reservation in any language on the same document or in a separate document to be attached.

WRITINGS OF SOVIET JURISTS

By the mid-1930's, the Soviet Union had established a comprehensive system of legislative and treaty norms regulating the passage of foreign merchant vessels and warships which relegated to the coastal state an unprecedented degree of discretion and jurisdiction over passing vessels. With the recognition of international custom as a legitimate though subordinate source of international law, Soviet jurists attempted to explain or reconcile the customary and legislative norms of innocent passage. Their efforts by no means produced identical results and reflected both differences of legal analysis and the changing requirements of Soviet foreign and commercial policy.

Innocent passage was not specifically treated in Soviet textbooks on maritime law during the 1920's and early 1930's.[9] In 1936 Sheptovitskii wrote that the right of innocent passage was "a generally recognized principle of the regime of territorial waters." Innocent passage was defined as "navigation not violating the rules established in the maritime belt for the safety of navigation nor the political and economic interests of the coastal state." "Political and economic interests" included the right to declare areas prohibited to vessels under national or foreign flags, but not "in general to prohibit the innocent passage of foreign vessels."[10]

In the 1950's Soviet legal treatises dealt with innocent passage at greater length. There were wide differences of opinion both as to the existence of a right of innocent passage and as to the attendant privileges and duties if its existence were acknowledged. G. I. Imenitov, writing in a 1951 maritime law textbook, made the unqualified statement that "the passage of foreign merchant vessels through territorial waters may not be prohibited by the coastal state," distinguishing "passage" from the "entry" of a vessel into port, which may be categorically prohibited by the coastal state.[11]

A more carefully considered and authoritative definition was given by V. N. Durdenevskii, who observed that the practice of states and international legal custom recognized a right of innocent passage for foreign merchant vessels through territorial waters. This right, however, Durdenevskii delimited in accordance with the provisions of the Soviet legislation cited above.[12]

A contrary position was adopted by Nikolaev:

> It is commonly stated in courses of international law that the authority of the coastal state in territorial waters is limited by the so-called right of innocent passage of foreign vessels, both merchant and military. . . this view can never be deemed correct, as it contradicts the sovereignty of the state over territorial waters and gives an opportunity to aggressive blocs to commit hostile actions against the coastal state under the guise of the "right of innocent passage".[13]

Nikolaev referred to the "admittance" (dopusk) of foreign vessels to Soviet territorial waters and concluded that:

> (F)oreign nonmilitary vessels may freely pass through the territorial waters of a coastal state if this passage is not only innocent, but is necessary from the viewpoint of customary navigation; but the coastal state may legally prohibit the navigation of foreign nonmilitary vessels in its territorial waters if this navigation is not called for by navigational necessity.[14]

Keilin concluded that "coastal states extend the right of innocent passage through territorial waters to the merchant vessels of other nations."[15] He described the provisions respecting innocent passage proposed at the 1930 Hague Conference for the Codification of International Law and then set forth the relevant Soviet legislative provisions. Although this point is not explicit, one may legitimately infer from Keilin's manner of presentation that he regarded the Hague rules as a valid reflection, in general, of international practice and that he viewed Soviet legislation as being consistent with these rules.

Bakhov adopted an equivocal position on the question of innocent passage, noting that "Soviet legislation does not prohibit the admittance of foreign merchant vessels into USSR territorial waters" and concluding that Soviet legislation is in accordance with generally recognized principles of international law. Foreign vessels, stated the manual, must follow a recommended course of navigation, avoid closed zones, and strictly observe the rules of fortified zones. The USSR is said to have an undisputed right of jurisdiction over foreign nonmilitary vessels found in its territorial waters. A distinction was drawn between merchant and trade (promyslovoi) ships. The latter are subject to being detained for engaging in fishing or other aquatic trade without proper documents or for conducting their trade by illegal means.[16]

A 1957 international law textbook contained important changes. The customary element of innocent passage received a different emphasis in a new formulation: "International practice shows that coastal countries do not customarily make the innocent passage of foreign merchant vessels through their territorial waters subject to special permission."[17] The word "right" (pravo) was no longer used in connection with passage; states were described as permitting innocent passage and as exercising their "rights" in regulating or prohibiting such passage.

The Geneva Convention on the Territorial Sea and Contiguous Zone, concluded in 1958, was ratified by the Presidium of the USSR Supreme Soviet on October 20, 1960; it entered into force on October 1, 1964.[18] The Soviet Union acceded to the Convention with two reservations.[19] Despite Soviet adherence to the Convention, Soviet jurists writing in 1960 and later continued to express diverse conceptions of innocent passage. Rodionov[20] and Shmigelskii[21] acknowledged, without any reference whatsoever to the Geneva Convention, that states may not hinder the innocent passage of merchant vessels nor interfere in the internal order of a passing ship. Lisovskii based his discussion of innocent passage on Soviet legislation and the 1930 Hague Conference.[22]

Other jurists quoted Article 15 of the 1960 statute on the state boundary as being dispositive, without reference to the Geneva Convention.[23] A. N. Siling,[24] A. K. Zhudro,[25] and N. I. Petrenko,[26] however, acknowledged that the legal regime of territorial waters is regulated at present by the Geneva agreement.

Extensive analyses of innocent passage and the Geneva Convention are found in a specialized monograph by A. L. Kolodkin and an essay by P. D. Barabolia. Kolodkin's treatment is basically descriptive of the correlative rights and duties of the coastal state and the passing vessel. He stressed the necessity for strict observance of a coastal state's laws and regulations in order for a passage to be innocent. The chief purpose of the rights and duties of the coastal state and of the passing vessel, writes Kolodkin, is the protection of the innocent character of a passage. Thus, the vessel's master is obliged to ensure that no act is committed by the vessel which in any degree infringes upon the political or defense interests of a coastal state and which could result in straining the relations between the vessel's state and the state to which the territorial waters belong.[27]

This obligation is in addition to that provided by Article 17 of the Geneva Convention requiring passing vessels to observe laws and rules of the coastal state and other norms of international law. Kolodkin does not indicate the source of his paramount obligation.

Barabolia's essay is more historical and analytical. He is the first Soviet writer to acknowledge that the right of innocent passage of nonmilitary vessels in territorial waters has been recognized in international law by the majority of states since "feudal" times. However, he criticized bourgeois theories which regard innocent passage as a "universal" and "unrestricted" right. These erroneous views are the result of regarding the territorial sea as part of the high seas instead of being under the sovereignty of the coastal state. Barabolia considered the provisions of the 1960 statute on the state boundary to be in full accordance with the Geneva Convention.[28]

Several jurists have accepted the distinction made in the 1956 naval international law manual between merchant vessels and trade vessels; the latter include vessels engaged in commercial fishing and hunting. Shmigelskii concluded in 1959 that foreign maritime trade vessels which did not have the right to conduct their trade in Soviet territorial waters might enter those waters only in the event of distress of storm, damage, or when sailing to or returning from their areas of trade.[29] Sobakin and also Shmigelskii find additional support for this distinction in Article 19 of the 1960 statute on the state boundary.[30] Functionally, their distinction is valid, but it is impossible of reconciliation with the Geneva Convention, which makes no such distinction, and with the generally accepted view that fishing vessels enjoy the right of innocent passage under the Convention. Having granted states the right to prohibit foreign maritime trade vessels from operating in territorial waters, there is no compelling reason to limit their passage or to assume their passage is not innocent unless it falls into the categories suggested by Shmigelskii. The 1966 naval international law manual moved away from Shmigelskii's view, noting that foreign fishing vessels have the right of innocent passage unless they violate rules prohibiting fishing in territorial waters.[31]

PASSAGE OF FOREIGN WARSHIPS IN TERRITORIAL WATERS

In contrast to the diversity of opinion with respect to merchant vessels, Soviet jurists are of one mind on the question of previous authorization from the coastal state for the passage of foreign warships through its territorial waters.[32] They contend that no generally recognized, obligatory international rules exist with respect to the right of innocent passage of foreign warships.

Contemporary writers have had difficulty establishing the existence of the principle of previous authorization in early Soviet practice. Pursuant to the 1927 statute on the state boundary, Provisional Rules for Foreign Warships Visiting USSR Waters were promulgated on March 28, 1931.[33] The Rules required previous authorization. Consent for a visit by a foreign warship was to be obtained through diplomatic channels, and certain information about the vessel, ports of call, purpose of passage, and length of stay was required. Warships carrying heads of state or diplomatic missions accredited to the USSR were exempt from some provisions. But despite the inclusion of "USSR waters" in the title of the Rules, they in fact applied only to arrivals of foreign warships in Soviet ports and internal waters. M. Ia. Sheptovitskii, while noting that warships represent the armed forces of a state and as a rule have not been subject to maritime law, was forced to conclude that authorization is necessary to enter internal waters.[34] V. N. Durdenevskii stated:

> Foreign warships also may pass in territorial waters without receiving previous authorization for this and without a previous notification about the passage. . . The practice of states shows that in peacetime states generally do not hinder the passage of foreign warships in their territorial waters.[35]

A. D. Keilin and P.P. Vinogradov, writing in 1939, expressed the view that previous consent of the coastal state must be received. Their opinion was often cited by Soviet international law textbooks published in the 1950's as a correct but not generally accepted position.[36]

The most ambitious attempt to base the principle of previous authorization in Soviet state practice was made by Nikolaev. Conceding the Provisional Rules were not explicit, he commented: ". . . it is possible to conclude from the general intent of these Rules that the authorization procedure provided by them relates to territorial waters inasmuch as they are a part of USSR waters."[37] Nikolaev also referred to other official Soviet documents, such as the Note of December 11, 1924, to U.S. Secretary of State Hughes protesting that the "entrance of an American warship into the territorial waters of the Soviet Union without corresponding authorization. . . contradicts international law."[38]

Keilin approved the doctrine of previous consent on the ground that the coastal state has no interest in having foreign warships pass that is comparable to the commercial advantages accruing from the passage of merchant vessels.[39]

The Draft Treaty on the Territorial Sea and Contiguous Zone submitted by the International Law Commission to the General Assembly contained an article permitting the coastal state to make the passage of warships through the territorial sea subject to previous authorization or notification.[40] This article was deleted from the final Convention over the strenuous objections of the Soviet Union.[41] The USSR has taken several measures to consolidate its position on this question.

First, it entered a reservation to Article 23 of the Convention. Second, it explicitly provided for a procedure of authorization for foreign warships in Article 16 of the 1960 statute on the state boundary and replaced the ambiguous Provisional Rules of 1931 regulating visits by foreign warships with a new set of Rules in 1960.[42]

Under the 1960 Rules, consent for the passage of foreign warships into Soviet territorial waters must be requested through diplomatic channels thirty days prior to the proposed visit. The request must specify the number, class, and name of the ship, the proposed port of call, the purpose of the passage, the length of stay in port, the rank and name of the commander, and the number and types of aircraft. Maximum duration of a visit is seven days, unless extended by special permission. No more than three vessels may enter any one port or area of territorial waters at the same time. Foreign warships in Soviet territorial waters are prohibited from conducting research, surveys, and also soundings, except those which are necessary in channels open to all navigation, from making photographs, drawings, sketches, or lists of port areas and fortifications, from sending out armed launches, sloops, or ship's boats, from firing any kind of weapon (except for salutes), laying or sweeping mines, using smoke screens, creating artificial fog or any type of underwater explosion, and from polluting waters. These provisions also apply to naval auxiliary vessels and armed ships for the protection of fisheries. A first violation of any of the provisions entails a warning; a second or a continuing offense, a request to leave Soviet waters. Foreign warships carrying heads of state or heads of diplomatic representations accredited to the Government of the USSR follow a procedure of notification rather than of authorization.

These Rules do not apply to foreign warships seeking refuge because of damage or distress of storm; however, compulsory pilotage regulations do apply in all instances.

Special attention was directed in the 1966 naval international law manual to the provisions requiring foreign submarines to navigate exclusively on the surface and to observe the rules for entry established for surface warships. Violation of either requirement is labeled a grave infringement of Soviet sovereignty and of generally recognized norms of international law. Because of observed instances of foreign submarines entering Soviet territorial waters for purposes of reconnaissance, the "Soviet Ministry of Defense has issued instructions that henceforth foreign submarines discovered violating the state boundary of the USSR and in a submerged position shall be destroyed."[43]

Soviet jurists have rejected the notion that the deletion of Draft Article 24 from the final Geneva Convention implies that foreign warships have the right to unhindered passage through territorial waters. Barabolia observed that Article 23 of the Convention, setting forth the conditions in which a coastal state may require a warship to leave the territorial sea, defined only the duties of warships and not their rights.[44] Petrenko urged that since Article 17 of the Convention requires the observance of laws and rules of the coastal state relating to transport and navigation and Article 23 requires foreign warships to observe the rules of the coastal state, these rules may include the requirement of previous authorization or previous notification. Moreover, the Convention did not exclude a procedure of authorization for foreign warships.[45]

SOVIET LEGISLATION AND THE GENEVA CONVENTION

The Chairman of the Soviet delegation to the Geneva Conference on the Law of the Sea summarized the results of the Geneva Convention with respect to the right of innocent passage as follows:

> It is generally recognized under international law that merchant and other non-military vessels have the right of unhindered passage through the territorial waters of a foreign state, provided they use the customary shipping routes. The coastal state has the right to lay down any rules it wishes regarding the passage of warships, including a requirement that preliminary notification be given or permission obtained.[46]

This interpretation of the Convention was subsequently embodied in the legislation enacted in 1960, previously described. Potential difficulties in reconciling the Soviet legislation with the Geneva Convention arise in at least two respects.

Article 15 of the statute on the state boundary considers passage innocent if vessels "follow a customary navigational course or a course recommended by competent agencies."

This clause imposes two conditions on a passing vessel, apparently under the authority of Article 17 of the Geneva Convention which provides that foreign vessels shall comply with the laws and regulations of the coastal state. The International Law Commission declined to specify the types of rules which might be enacted under Article 17 because such a list could not be exhaustive; it did mention "use of the route prescribed for international navigation", presumably meaning that route prescribed by the coastal state.[47] This seems to dispose of the first half of the clause. But what is a course "recommended by competent agencies?" Barabolia stated that "generally recommended courses" are established in places dangerous for navigation, near sandbars, submerged rocks, and approaches to ports.[48] If "generally recommended course" is interpreted merely to refer to authorized deviations from the customary navigational course, it is consistent with the Convention. However, a broader application of the phrase by Soviet authorities could lead to actions contrary to the Convention.

A serious potential discrepancy with the Convention arises under Article 16 of the 1960 statute, which prescribes the procedure of authorization for the passage of foreign warships through Soviet territorial waters. That warships have a right of innocent passage under the text of the Convention is a reasonable interpretation, although it may be and has been argued that the majority of delegates did not intend warships to have this right.[49] Article 14 under Subsection A: "Rules Applicable to All Ships" states that "ships of all states. . . shall enjoy the right of innocent passage. . ." There is no restriction on warships; Article 14, paragraph 6 specifically directs that one type of warship, the submarine, navigate on the surface. The fact that many nations filed reservations when the article permitting states to require previous authorization was deleted from the Convention strongly suggests that they recognized that the deletion amounted to approval of the right of passage.

Soviet legislation operates in effect to deny the right of innocent passage to warships rather than to restrict that right. The requirement of thirty days advance notice of the proposed passage and the discretion to withhold authorization transform the passage of warships in Soviet territorial waters into a privilege. Even were the requirement of authorization dispensed with, thirty days notice would effectively limit the right of passage in violation of the Convention.[50]

The position of the USSR on this problem is probably motivated by considerations of defense, by the fact that international maritime routes do not pass through Soviet territorial waters (although technological developments could transform the Northern Sea Route into a major international shipping route), and by the belief that widespread acceptance of their position would diminish the predominance of Western sea and air power in many parts of the world (it would equally restrict the application of formidable Soviet naval power). The support for the Soviet view of many nations at the Geneva Conference which did not enter reservations to Article 23 suggests that no international consensus has been reached on the passage of warships notwithstanding a strict reading of the Convention. The pronounced tendency of the 1958 Convention to favor extensions of the coastal states' sovereignty over the territorial sea will no doubt continue to be reflected in state practice with respect to the innocent passage of warships through territorial waters.

NOTES

1. See Butler, "Soviet Concepts of Innocent Passage," 7 Harvard International Law Journal 113-130 (1965).

2. Peace Treaty Between Russia and Finland, October 14, 1920. 3 Dokumenty 277.

3. See Peace Treaty Between Russia and Estonia, February 2, 1920. 2 Dokumenty 339; Peace Treaty Between Russia and Latvia, August 11, 1920. 3 Dokumenty 101.

4. 3 Meshera, Morskoe pravo: pravovoi rezhim morskikh putei (Maritime Law; Legal Regime of Maritime Routes) 6 (1959).

5. SU RSFSR (1921), no. 49, item 259; Prikaz RVSR of December 28, 1921, no. 2933.

6. SU RSFSR (1923), no. 6, item 93; SU RSFSR (1922), no. 61, item 780.

7. Quoted by P. D. Barabolia in Koretskii and Tunkin, Ocherki mezhdunarodnogo morskogo prava (Outlines of International Maritime Law) 109 (1962).

8. SZ SSSR (1927), no. 62, item 625. Portions of the Statute are translated in United Nations Legislative Series, Laws and Regulations on the Regime of the Territorial Sea 255-258 (1957).

9. The first Soviet treatise on maritime law appears to be Rykachev, Morskoe torgovoe pravo (Maritime Commercial Law) (1928).

10. Sheptovitskii, Morskoe pravo (Maritime Law) 34 (1936). The same view was expressed by Pashukanis, Ocherki po mezhdunarodnomu pravu (Outlines of International Law) 120 (1935).

11. Imenitov, Sovetskoe morskoe i rybolovnoe pravo (Soviet Maritime and Fishing Law) 21 (1951).

12. Korovin, Mezhdunarodnoe pravo (International Law) 302-303 (1951).

13. Nikolaev, Problema territorialnykh vod v mezhdunarodnom prave (Problem of Territorial Waters in International Law) 47 (1954).

14. Id. at 51.

15. Keilin, Sovetskoe morskoe pravo (Soviet Maritime Law) 62 (1954).

16. Bakhov, Voenno-morskoi mezhdunarodno-pravovoi spravochnik (Naval International Law Manual) 85-87 (1956).

17. Kozhevnikov, Mezhdunarodnoe pravo (International Law) 210 (1957).

18. The official Russian text is published in Vedomosti SSSR (1964), no. 43, item 472.

19. To Article 20: "The Government of the USSR considers that state ships in foreign territorial waters enjoy immunity and therefore the application of measures mentioned in the present article may occur only with the consent of the state under whose flag the vessel sails".

To Article 23: (Subsection D. The Rule Applying to Warships) "The Government of the USSR considers that a coastal state has the right to establish a procedure of authorization for the passage of foreign warships through its territorial waters". *Ibid.*

20. Levin and Kaliuzhnaia, *Mezhdunarodnoe pravo (International Law)* 168 (1960).

21. Shmigelskii and Iasinovskii, *Osnovy sovetskogo morskogo prava (Fundamental Principles of Soviet Maritime Law)* 30 (1959).

22. Lisovskii, *Mezhdunarodnoe pravo (International Law)* 154-156 (2d ed. 1961).

23. Shmigelskii and Iasinovskii, *Osnovy sovetskogo morskogo prava (Fundamental Principles of Soviet Maritime Law)* 33-35 (1963); Kozhevnikov, *Mezhdunarodnoe pravo (International Law)* 218 (1964).

24. Siling, *Morskoe pravo (Maritime Law)* 60-62 (1964).

25. Zhudro, *et. al.*, *Morskoe pravo (Maritime Law)* 94 (1964).

26. Levin and Kaliuzhnaia, *Mezhdunarodnoe pravo (International Law)* 195 (1964).

27. Kolodkin, *Pravovoi rezhim territorialnykh vod i otkrytogo moria (The Legal Regime of Territorial Waters and the High Seas)* 32 (1961).

28. Koretskii and Tunkin, *op. cit. supra* note 7.

29. Shmigelskii, *op. cit. supra* note 21, at 31.

30. Levin and Kaliuzhnaia, *op. cit. supra* note 26, at 220; Shmigelskii, *op. cit. supra* note 23 above, at 33.

31. Barabolia, et. al., Voenno-morskoi mezhdunarodno-pravovoi spravochnik (Naval International Law Manual) 31 (1966).

32. Article 35 of the 1964 Customs Code defines a warship as "any vessel (or auxiliary vessel) sailing under a military or border guard flag, under the command of a person in military service and on the staff of a military command, as well as a vessel which in accordance with a special statement of the USSR Ministry of Defense, performs tasks of a military-operational nature. The Commander of a warship bears responsibility for observing the provisions of the Customs Code." Article 36 extends the provisions of Article 35 to foreign warships visiting USSR ports. Vedomosti SSSR (1964), no. 20, item 242.

33. The full text of the Provisional Rules is reproduced in Bakhov, op. cit. supra note 16, at 106-109. Harben erroneously referred to "undisclosed" Soviet rules relating to warships.

34. Sheptovitskii, op. cit. supra note 10, at 51.

35. Durdenevskii and Krylov, Mezhdunarodnoe pravo (International Law) 257 (1947).

36. See Kozhevnikov, op. cit. supra note 17, at 212.

37. Nikolaev, op. cit. supra note 13, at 214.

38. Note from the People's Commissariat for Foreign Affairs of the USSR to Secretary of State Hughes of the USA, December 11, 1924. 7 Dokumenty 572-573; (1924) Foreign Relations U.S. 681.

39. Keilin, op. cit. supra note 15, at 64.

40. (1956), 2 Yb. Int'l L. Comm. 276 (A/CN.4/SER.A/1956/Add.1) (1957).

41. Tunkin urged that foreign warships cannot pass without the consent of the coastal state because that would

entail a security risk for the latter and had in practice given rise to abuse. 3 U.N. Conf. on Law of the Sea 32 (1958).

42. The official text of the 1960 Rules has been published annually in the first issue of Izveshcheniia moreplavateliam, a weekly publication of the Soviet Naval Hydrographic Service in Leningrad, attached to the USSR Ministry of Defense. Subsequent weekly issues of the Izveshcheniia, which translated into English is Notices to Mariners, contain technical navigational information and corrections to Soviet charts and publications. It is published in the same format and size as Vedomosti SSSR. The United States Naval Oceanographic Office appears to be the sole American recipient. Soviet jurists often cite different years of the Izveshcheniia when discussing the Rules. The Rules also are reproduced in Barabolia, op. cit. supra note 31, at 69-75.

43. Barabolia, ibid. at 50; regulations governing signals by submarines in distress are published in IM (1966), no. 7.

44. Koretskii and Tunkin, op. cit. supra note 7.

45. Levin and Kaliuzhnaia, op. cit. supra note 26, at 195.

46. Tunkin, "The Geneva Conference on the Law of the Sea," 1958 International Affairs (M), no. 7, p. 48.

47. Op. cit. supra note 40, at 274.

48. Koretskii and Tunkin, op. cit. supra note 7, at 110.

49. Sorenson, "The Law of the Sea," International Conciliation, no. 520, 244 (1958); Jessup, "The United Nations Conference on the Law of the Sea," 59 Columbia Law Review 234-268 (1959).

50. A Soviet delegate to the 1958 Geneva Conference on the Law of the Sea, A. N. Nikolaev, met this objection by arguing that "the paramount interests of a state should not be subordinated to a desire for haste in some other quarters." 3 U.N. Conf. on Law of the Sea 130 (1958).

CHAPTER 6 CRIMINAL AND CIVIL JURISDICTION

There is no special law in the Soviet Union regulating criminal jurisdiction in territorial waters. Article 4 of the 1958 All-Union Fundamental Principles of Criminal Legislation extended the full scope of territorial jurisdiction to "all persons who commit crimes on the territory of the USSR."[1] Inasmuch as Soviet territorial waters are under the full sovereignty of the Soviet Union, this Article applies to all crimes committed on board foreign vessels while in waters of the USSR. On its face, Article 4 is inconsistent with a decree of May 24, 1927, which governs the procedure of arrests on foreign merchant vessels:

> Appropriate authorities of the RSFSR shall have the right to make arrests of criminals on foreign merchant vessels only in those instances when the crime was committed by them wholly or partly on the shore or when the consequences of these crimes may give rise to serious complications on shore.[2]

However, Soviet authorities customarily refrain from interfering, in accordance with international practice, if the crime committed does not threaten the security or public order of the Soviet Union or the humane principles of Soviet socialist law.[3]

The Criminal Code of the RSFSR contains numerous provisions directly pertaining to the regime of territorial waters: smuggling (Art. 78); illegal exit abroad or illegal entry into the USSR (Art. 83); violation of rules of safe movement and operation of transport (Art. 85); damaging routes of communication and means of transport (Art. 86); failure of master of vessel to render aid to victim of disaster (Art. 129); violation of veterinary rules (Art. 160); violation of rules established for combating plant diseases and pests (Art. 161); illegally engaging in fishing or other water extractive trades (Art. 163); illegally engaging in hunting of seals and beavers (Art. 164); blasting in violation of rules for protection of fish reserves (Art. 165); illegal hunting (Art. 166); illegal displaying of state flag of USSR or union republic on merchant vessel (Art. 203); failure to render aid upon collision of vessel or failure to communicate name of vessel (Art. 204); damaging of marine telegraph cable (Art. 205); violation of rules governing transport (Art. 213); and violation of rules established for the purpose of combating epidemics (Art. 222).

The 1960 statute on the state boundary empowered ships and other vessels of the border guard to detain any foreign nonmilitary vessel situated in the territorial or internal waters of the Soviet Union or in the Soviet part of the waters of border rivers and lakes and to convoy it to the nearest port or harbor when: (a) the vessel is situated in regions permanently or temporarily closed for navigation as announced in Notices to Mariners; (b) the vessel embarks or disembarks people or loads or unloads cargo in places not established for this purpose if these actions are performed without the permission of competent agencies; (c) the vessel illegally engages in maritime or river trade or hydrographic work and research in Soviet territorial and internal waters; (d) the officers or crew of vessels deliberately damage navigational barriers, cables, or other submerged or protruding objects belonging to the USSR; (e) the vessel's master does not present ship or cargo documents; (f) the vessel refuses to submit to instructions of appropriate authorities of the Soviet Union; and (g) in other instances when the vessel is in Soviet territorial waters, internal waters, border rivers and lakes in violation of the 1960 statute.[4]

Persons who have committed "criminal transgressions"[5] and who are subject to criminal responsibility under USSR and union republic legislation may be detained and taken from a vessel by the border guard unless the foreign vessel is passing through Soviet territorial waters, proceeding from a foreign port, and does not enter internal waters, and the crime was committed prior to the vessel's entering territorial waters.[6]

A. N. Nikolaev cited a 1940 Statute on the Procedure of Investigation of Maritime Average as extending USSR jurisdiction to territorial waters in that if during the course of an investigation the indicia of a criminal transgression are discovered, the chief of a port shall inform the procurator and may detain a foreign vessel in port.[7] However, the statute only mentions "waters" of the USSR, not territorial waters; it would seem to relate only to internal waters.

Foreign nonmilitary vessels may be detained by Soviet authorities for unseaworthiness if certain elementary safety requirements are not fulfilled.[8] Other legislation provides for administrative or criminal responsibility for violation of fishing, use of wireless radio equipment, customs, and sanitary rules.

No statistics are available with respect to the frequency of proceedings under the aforementioned legislation. Most of the reported offenses involve fishing violations. Soviet maritime law textbooks frequently mention the arrests and convictions of British fishing trawlers during the 1920's and again in the early 1950's. Other incidents involving Norwegian, Danish, Swedish, and Japanese citizens have been reported by Western media. The translation of the Soviet court decision in the case of the St. Hubert in the documentary appendix is probably not untypical of the usual proceeding.[9]

Civil jurisdiction is exercised under the 1961 All-Union Fundamental Principles of Civil Legislation, the union republic civil codes, and special legislation relating to civil law and foreign trade relations[10] in accordance with Article 20 of the 1958 Geneva Convention on the Territorial Sea.

Foreign warships enjoy extraterritoriality in Soviet territorial waters. No action of an administrative or judicial character may be taken against them for violations of Soviet legislation and rules.

RIGHT OF HOT PURSUIT

The right of hot pursuit from Soviet territorial waters is defined by Article 36 of the 1960 statute on the state boundary. The border guard of the USSR may continue to pursue non-military foreign vessels onto the high seas, if the pursuit began in Soviet territorial or internal waters and is conducted without interruption, until the vessel enters its own territorial waters or those of a foreign state.

NOTES

1. The RSFSR Criminal Code incorporates the provisions of Article 4 of the 1958 All-Union Fundamental Principles of Criminal Legislation. The other union republic codes contain similar provisions. See Berman and Spindler, trans., *Soviet Criminal Law and Procedure: The RSFSR Codes* 146 (1966).

2. *SU RSFSR* (1927), no. 52, item 348.

3. Zhudro, *et. al.*, *Morskoe pravo* (*Maritime Law*) 108 (1964).

4. Article 37, Statute on Protection of the State Boundary of the USSR, August 5, 1960, *Vedomosti SSSR* (1960), no. 34, item 324; the Rules for Hoisting Signals by Border Guard Ships in order to Stop Nonmilitary Vessels in Territorial and Internal Waters of the USSR are published in *IM* (1966), no. 2.

5. "*Ugolovnoe prestuplenie*", literally a "criminal crime". This formulation appears to exclude the detention of persons for committing offenses which are only administratively punishable.

6. Article 36, *op. cit.* *supra* note 4.

7. Prikaz of the People's Commissariat for the Merchant Marine, no. 190, April 15, 1940.

8. 3 Meshera, Morskoe pravo: pravovoi rezhim morskikh putei (Maritime Law; Legal Regime of Maritime Routes) 28 (1959).

9. Consul Grout to Secretary of State Hughes, March 23, 1922, MS. National Archives, file 361.4154Sa2/-, containing a translation of the decision of the Soviet court, March 1922.

10. The 1964 RSFSR Civil Code is translated in Gray, Soviet Civil Legislation (1965); Kiralfy, The Civil Code and the Code of Civil Procedure of the RSFSR 1964 (1966). Also see sections 2, 239, and 240 of the Merchant Shipping Code of the Soviet Union.

CHAPTER 7 SPECIAL ZONES

The Soviet attitude towards the theory of contiguous zones has been closely related to that of territorial waters. Those writers who interpreted Soviet legislation as extending jurisdiction for particular purposes explained that extension in terms of contiguous zones. Imenitov, for example, stated that the 1935 decree on fishing established a contiguous zone in which fishing by foreign vessels was prohibited.[1] Similarly, on August 13, 1925, the Baltic states, including the USSR, signed a convention designed to curtail the smuggling of alcoholic beverages in which enforcement authority for this purpose was extended to twelve miles from shore.[2] Belli's interpretation of the entire prewar pattern of Soviet maritime legislation was based on the theory of contiguous zones, and non-Soviet writers have drawn similar conclusions independently.[3] The 1947 international law textbook stated that there was no international rule on the breadth of contiguous zones.[4]

At the present time all Soviet jurists appear to accept the doctrine of full sovereignty of the Soviet state over its territorial waters. "In the USSR there are no contiguous zones in the common understanding of that term."[5] However, there is unresolved disagreement with respect to the status of fishing zones. Siling has pointed out that the fishing zone has an independent significance differing from the contiguous zone in that the former protects exclusively the economic interests of the coastal state whereas the latter involves the legal order. Fishing zones may be established irrespective of the breadth of the territorial sea, freedom of commercial navigation, and innocent passage. A foreign vessel has rights in a contiguous zone, but a fishing zone establishes special rights which belong only to the vessels and citizens of the coastal state.[6] Zhudro, expressing a contrary view, discussed fishing zones under the subdivision "contiguous zones" and noted that in practice states widely exercise the right to establish such zones even though the fishing zone is not expressly mentioned in the 1958 Geneva Convention on the Territorial Sea.[7]

Most of the headings below would be subsumed in a Western international law treatise under the section on contiguous zones. In Soviet literature these are regarded as rights which a coastal state may exercise within its territorial waters. With the exception of cabotage, which is not commonly regarded by Western jurists as a corollary of sovereignty over territorial waters, we discuss below those rights mentioned in Soviet literature, bearing in mind that Soviet publicists do not regard this list as necessarily an exhaustive one.

FISHING ZONE

The Constitution of the USSR provides that "the land, its mineral wealth, waters . . . are state property, that is, belong to the whole people."[8] Thus all the riches in the seabed of territorial waters and within those waters which have been discovered or may be discovered in the future belong exclusively to the Soviet state. The exclusive right to fishing and other maritime trades within the limits of Soviet territorial waters is reserved to Soviet organizations and citizens. Commercial fishing and hunting have been an important source of income and food supply to the Soviet state.

The conduct of maritime trade (fishing, crabbing, hunting of sea furbearing animals, and any other trade) in Soviet territorial waters is forbidden to foreign vessels unless provided otherwise by an international agreement with the Soviet Union. Foreign vessels violating this rule, or having permission to engage in maritime trade but conducting it in violation of the established rules, are subject to detention, and persons guilty of so doing are subject to administrative and criminal penalties under USSR and union republic legislation.[9]

Pursuant to a 1958 Decree Concerning the Conservation of Fishery Resources and the Regulation of Fishing in the Waters of the USSR, all waters of the USSR which are used or which may be used for the commerical extraction of fish and other marine life and growth or which have significance for the reproduction of reserves of fish constitute the economic fishery reserves of the USSR.[10] Fishery conservation agencies of the union republics or border guard agencies are responsible for enforcing these rules. Articles 163-166 of the 1960 RSFSR Criminal Code contain severe penalties for illegally engaging in fishing or other water extractive trade, hunting seals or beavers, blasting in violation of rules for the protection of fish reserves, and illegal hunting.

As has been noted previously, Russia established a twelve-mile fishing zone on the Pacific coast in 1911. The USSR extended this zone to the northern sea coast and the White Sea by a decree of May 24, 1921.[11] Exclusive fishing rights in all Soviet territorial waters were unequivocally asserted in a 1935 decree on fishing.[12] This decree was superseded in 1954,[13] although some Soviet jurists have referred to it as being in force.[14] Confusion exists as to whether the 1954 decree has, in turn, been supplanted by a new decree of 1958.[15]

The Soviet Government made definite claims to a twelve-mile fishing zone in the series of prewar fishing regulations commencing in 1921. The decrees were vigorously protested by Great Britain, Norway, Germany, and Japan. A number of serious incidents involving foreign fishing trawlers in Soviet waters occurred during the 1920's. The effects of these decrees were virtually nullified by bilateral treaties and informal agreements with the protesting states. Under a provisional agreement concerning fishing of May 22, 1930, between the USSR and Great Britain, British fishing vessels were permitted to operate within three miles of the northern coasts of the USSR and in specified portions of the White Sea. The agreement expressly did not constitute recognition or non-recognition of the Soviet twelve-mile claim.[16] This privilege extended to Germany and Norway by virtue of most-favored-nation provisions in treaties signed by the USSR in 1925 with those states.[17] Analogous arrangements were made with Japan in 1925 and 1928.[18]

Fishing agreements were difficult to obtain from the Soviet Union after 1945. The 1930 agreement with Great Britain was denounced in 1953 and temporarily renewed for 1954 and 1955. A new agreement with Britain, concluded for a five year period and signed May 25, 1956, entering into force March 12, 1957, was denounced by the Soviet Union on March 12, 1961, and lost force one year from that date pursuant to the denunciation clause in the agreement.[19]

At the present time there are three agreements between the Soviet Union and neighboring states which give foreign citizens limited fishing rights in Soviet territorial waters. In an agreement with Finland of February 21, 1959, the Soviet Government agreed to permit Finnish citizens resident in certain communes adjacent to the Soviet border the right to engage in fishing and sealing in the territorial waters of the Soviet Union in the Gulf of Finland in areas delimited by the agreement.[20]

Under the terms of a 1962 agreement between the Soviet Union and Norway, Norwegian fishermen are permitted to engage in fishing in Soviet territorial waters in the Varanger Fiord until October 31, 1970. The agreement contains rules governing the conduct of reciprocal fishing rights. Apart from these fishing regulations, Norwegian nationals and vessels in Soviet territorial waters are subject to Soviet laws.[21]

In 1963 the Soviet Union concluded an agreement with the Japan Fisheries Association permitting certain fishermen to engage in the gathering of sea kale near the Island of Kaigara. The area is strictly delimited by buoys. The number of vessels in the area may not exceed three hundred, and the length of the annual season is three and one half months. The Japan Fisheries Association pays the Soviet side 12,000 Japanese yen for each vessel taking part in the trade.[22] Nonetheless, Japan has been unable to achieve a satisfactory arrangement for access to Soviet territorial waters along the Pacific coast, although the recently signed Soviet-Japanese consular agreement may improve the legal protection of Japanese fishermen in Soviet territorial waters.[23] Soviet claims to the Sea of Japan and the Okhotsk Sea as closed are strongly influenced by the immense fishery resources in those areas.

REGULATION OF NAVIGATION

Competent agencies of the USSR may establish districts in separate portions of Soviet territorial waters in which the navigation, anchoring, or conduct of maritime trade by vessels is prohibited. The establishment of such zones is announced in Notices to Mariners.[24] Article 22 of the Law on State Crimes imposes criminal responsibility for the violation of rules for the safe movement and use of water transport which results in an accident or in grave consequences.[25]

Pilot services are governed by Annex V of the Merchant Shipping Code of the Soviet Union.[26] The Ministry of the Maritime Fleet establishes the districts where the use of a Soviet pilot is compulsory. In certain zones the services of a pilot may be required even though the passing vessel is not proceeding to a Soviet port. Navigation along the coast near Vladivostok, for example, is permitted without a pilot only if vessels obtain instructions from the chief military pilot at Vladivostok.[27]

Icebreaker services are available in accordance with the rules published on September 14, 1944.[28]

USE OF WIRELESS RADIO EQUIPMENT

A Soviet decree of July 24, 1928, restricts the use of wireless radio equipment by warships and nonmilitary vessels within ten miles from shore in Soviet internal waters or the maritime sea belt. Nonmilitary vessels are prohibited from exchanging radio messages with shore stations unless they are in danger or are rendering aid to another vessel in distress or are being led through ice or must complete an especially important exchange with port authorities.[29]

All radio messages of warships and nonmilitary vessels must be open, without using any cypher or code except for international signal codes. The local commander of Soviet naval forces may restrict radio exchanges of foreign warships with respect to duration and wave length. Persons violating the decree are subject to Soviet criminal sanctions.

Until 1960, violation of the decree could entail punishment under Article 75-3 of the 1926 RSFSR Criminal Code. The 1960 RSFSR Criminal Code does not appear to contain an offense analogous to Article 75-3.

CUSTOMS

Article 23 of the 1960 statute on the state boundary provided that customs control over the state boundary shall be exercised by agencies of the USSR Ministry of Foreign Trade in accordance with prevailing legislation and agreements with other states.

A new USSR Customs Code became effective July 1, 1964.[30] Article 36 of the Code exempts foreign warships from customs inspection. All other foreign vessels are subject to customs inspection unless provided otherwise by international agreement. Under Article 21, customs control extends to vessels arriving in ports. In practice customs inspection is not conducted within territorial waters but in internal (port) waters, even though passengers and goods cross the state boundary upon entering territorial waters.

SANITARY PROTECTION

The Soviet Union applies the International Sanitary Rules adopted at the fourth assembly of the World Health Organization on May 25, 1951, as amended in 1955 and 1956. Sanitary protection of the Soviet state boundary is carried out by the USSR Ministry of Health Sanitary and Epidemiological Service in accordance with a Soviet decree of 1931[31] and rules adopted by the Ministry of Health on August 20, 1959.[32] In the event of a threat of an especially dangerous infection spreading in Soviet territory or in an adjacent state, the competent agencies are empowered to temporarily close the threatened portions of the boundary and to place a quarantine over the area.[33]

SALVAGE

Annex IX of the Merchant Shipping Code of the Soviet Union governs the salvage of sunken property in Soviet territorial waters.[34] The owner of sunken property is allowed one year to submit to the competent border guard agency a declaration of intention to raise the property. The declaration must specify a proposed time period for completing the salvage operations. The border guard agency may allow the owner sufficient time according to the circumstances of the situation. Salvage of Soviet-owned vessels or cargo is conducted exclusively by Soviet agencies.

REGIME OF AIRSPACE OVER TERRITORIAL WATERS

The regime of Soviet airspace is governed by the Air Code of the USSR,[35] instructions issued pursuant thereto by Soviet state agencies,[36] and international air agreements. Article 1 of the Code declares:

> The Union of Soviet Socialist Republics exercises full and exclusive sovereignty over airspace of the USSR.
>
> Airspace of the USSR shall mean the airspace above the land and water territory of the USSR, including territorial waters, as determined by USSR laws and international agreements concluded by the USSR.

The provisions of the Code are binding for all types of civil aviation and civil aeronautics within the limits of the Soviet Union.

The Soviet Union does not recognize a right of innocent passage for foreign aircraft over Soviet territorial waters.

Flights of foreign aircraft in Soviet airspace may be performed only in accordance with international air agreements to which the USSR is a party or on the basis of special authorization. In either case, international flights must follow established air lanes.

NOTES

1. Imenitov, Sovetskoe morskoe i rybolovnoe pravo (Soviet Maritime and Fishing Law) 21 (1951).

2. 42 LNTS 75.

3. See Ohira, "Fishing Problems Between Soviet Russia and Japan," 2 Japanese Annual of International Law 1-19 (1958).

4. Durdenevskii and Krylov, Mezhdunarodnoe pravo (International Law) 258 (1947).

5. Levin and Kaliuzhnaia, Mezhdunarodnoe pravo (International Law) 171 (1960). Koretskii contended the establishment of special zones was a circuitous means to extend sovereign rights. "Rights exercised in such zones were the same as those possessed by the coastal state in the territorial sea and the effort to justify those claims on the ground that they were necessary solely for purposes of administration, control and jurisdiction carried no weight because those were precisely the functions discharged by a state in virtue of its sovereignty." 3 U.N. Conf. on Law of the Sea 67 (1958).

6. Siling, Morskoe pravo (Maritime Law) 62 (1964); A. A. Volkov concurred: "Some authors erroneously equate the volume of rights of coastal states in the fishing and contiguous zones. In reality fishing zones are areas of special competence of coastal states in which their volume of rights is incomparably greater than in contiguous zones." Volkov, "Pravovoi rezhim rybolovnykh zon," (Legal Regime

of Fishing Zones) 1963 Sovetskii ezhegodnik mezhdunarodnogo prava (Soviet Yearbook of International Law) 218 (1965).

7. Zhudro, et. al., Morskoe pravo (Maritime Law) 114 (1964).

8. Article 6, Constitution of the USSR (1965 ed.).

9. Article 19, Statute on Protection of the State Boundary of the USSR, August 5, 1960, Vedomosti SSSR (1960), no. 34, item 324. Administrative penalties for violations of USSR fishing regulations were recently increased. See Vedomosti SSSR (1964), no. 14, item 158. Fishing legislation prior to 1937 is treated in Bohmert, "Die russische Fischereigrenze," 21 Zeitschrift fur Volkerrecht 441-496 (1937); 257-306 (1938).

10. SP SSSR (1958), no. 16, item 127; partially reproduced in Kolbasov, comp., Okhrana prirody: sbornik zakonodatelnykh aktov (Conservation: Collected Legislative Acts) (1961) and translated in 3 Soviet Statutes and Decisions, no. 1, at 56-57 (1966).

11. SU RSFSR (1921), no. 49, item 259.

12. SZ SSSR (1935), no. 50, item 420.

13. The only available text of the 1954 decree is an excerpt translated in United Nations Legislative Series, Laws and Regulations on the Regime of the Territorial Sea 577-578 (1957). Bakhov states that the 1954 decree repealed the 1935 decree. See Bakhov, Voenno-morskoi mezhdunarodno-pravovoi spravochnik (Naval International Law Manual) 188 (1956).

14. Lisovskii, Mezhdunarodnoe pravo (International Law) 155 (2d ed. 1961). Shmigelskii implied that both the 1935 and 1954 decrees are in force. See Shmigelskii and Iasinovskii, Osnovy sovetskogo morskogo prava (Fundamental Principles of Soviet Maritime Law) 33 (1963). Of the 390,000 decrees and regulations enacted by the USSR Council of Ministers between 1937 and 1958, only some thousands were published. The rest were distributed to the officials concerned with their enforcement and to other authorized persons. A 1958 edict on the publication of laws

required that decrees of the Council of Ministers which are of general significance or have a normative character be published in the SP. Foreigners may not subscribe to the SP, although it is available in libraries in the Soviet Union and is not considered classified information. Berman, Justice in the U.S.S.R. 76-77 (rev. ed. 1963); Berman and Spindler, Soviet Criminal Law and Procedure: The RSFSR Codes 405 (1966).

15. See 3 Meshera, Morskoe pravo: pravovoi rezhim morskikh putei (Maritime Law; Legal Regime of Maritime Routes) 21 (1959); Zhudro, op. cit. supra note 7, at 104. It would appear there is some disagreement as to whether the 1958 decree applies to both internal waters and territorial waters or merely the former.

16. 25 Martens, N.R.G. 3d ser. 143-145.

17. 53 LNTS 7-162; 48 LNTS 9-37.

18. 3 SDD 10-18; 15 Martens, N.R.G. 3d ser. 425-443. See Wertheim, "The Russo-Japanese Fisheries Controversy," 8 Pacific Affairs 185-198 (1935); Barnes, "Fisheries: Mainstay of Soviet-Japanese Friction," 9 Far Eastern Survey 75-80 (1940).

19. Barabolia, et. al., Voenno-morskoi mezhdunarodno-pravovoi spravochnik (Naval International Law Manual) 286 (1966).

20. Vedomosti SSSR (1959), no. 14, item 87. This agreement was extended on May 23, 1966. Vedomosti SSSR (1966), no. 22, item 388; 338 UNTS 3.

21. Vedomosti SSSR (1962), no. 34, item 362.

22. Barabolia, op. cit. supra note 19, at 238.

23. The draft convention is translated in 5 International Legal Materials 1144 (1966); 3 Soviet Statutes and Decisions, no. 2-3, at 127-149 (1967).

24. Article 9, 1960 statute, op. cit. supra note 9. Among the rules published in Notices to Mariners are:

Statute Concerning Areas Where Free Passage is Restricted and Rules of Navigation Therein, IM (1966), no. 3; Rules Concerning Distress Signals and Notices of Dangers to Navigation, IM (1966), no. 13; Announcement Concerning Mined Areas and Channels of Navigation Therein, IM (1966), no. 25.

25. Vedomosti SSSR (1959), no. 1, item 8.

26. The full text of the Merchant Shipping Code is translated in Documentation Office for East European Law, University of Leyden, Law in Eastern Europe -- The Merchant Shipping Code of the Soviet Union, no. 4 (1960). See also Dobrin, "A propos the Soviet Maritime Code," 49 Law Quarterly Review 249-267 (1933); Dobrin, "The Soviet Maritime Code, 1929," 16 Journal of Comparative Legislation 252-268 (1934); Keilin, "Le Droit Maritime de l'Union Sovietique," 11 Le Droit Maritime Francais 628-631 (1959).

27. Strohl, The International Law of Bays 334 (1963).

28. IM (1966), no. 15.

29. SZ SSSR (1928), no. 48, item 431.

30. Vedomosti SSSR (1964), no. 20, item 242; translated with reproduction of the Russian text in Butler, Customs Code of the USSR (1966).

31. SZ SSSR (1931), no. 55, item 355.

32. SP SSSR (1959), no. 13, item 80. Cited by Zhudro, op. cit. supra note 7, at 112. The 1959 rules evidently replace rules issued in 1940. No text of the new rules has been located. Zhudro is the only Soviet publicist since 1959 to cite them.

33. Article 23, 1960 statute, op. cit. supra note 9.

34. Op. cit. supra note 26, at 93-95.

35. Vedomosti SSSR (1961), no. 52, item 538; translated in Cooper, The Air Code of the U.S.S.R. (1966).

36. Flight Rules for Foreign Civil Aircraft Within the Territory of the USSR, _in_ 2 United States Senate Committee on Commerce, _Air Laws and Treaties of the World_ 2570 (1965).

CHAPTER 8 LEGAL NORMS APPLIED TO INDIVIDUAL SEAS

BALTIC SEA

The Baltic Sea indents deeply into the northwestern part of the European mainland. The Soviet shoreline is generally not unusually jagged except along the Gulf of Finland, where there are many rocky islands lining the labyrinth-like straits. The reef-formations characteristic of this coast are unknown to other seas and, as noted previously, have required the use of a different method for calculating territorial waters. Both the Gulf of Finland and the Riga Bay freeze during the winter.

The Baltic is the closest connection for the Soviet Union to the industrial markets of Europe and the world's major maritime routes, although the maritime routes of the Baltic itself have economic significance chiefly for the Baltic states. The Baltic Sea is also an important cabotage route between the Leningrad and Kaliningrad oblasts of the RSFSR and the Lithuanian and Estonian Union Republics.[1] Seven Baltic ports are open to foreign merchant vessels,[2] Leningrad and Riga being the most important in terms of cargo turnover.

The Soviet Union has had no traditional claims in the Baltic. Prior to World War II, the only Soviet coastline bordering the Baltic, along the Gulf of Finland, was administered jointly with Finland under the provisions of the Treaty of Dorpat of October 14, 1920. This treaty, containing important concessions on the part of the RSFSR, provided *inter alia* for the right of Finnish merchant vessels to sail on the Neva River to Lake Ladozh and back through Leningrad waters. It established a four-mile limit for territorial waters in the Gulf, except for certain islands where the limit was three miles.[3] Subsequent agreements regulated fishing, customs, detention procedures, and smuggling.[4] On August 3, 1930, the Soviet Union formally extended the authority of USSR and RSFSR agencies to

Soviet territorial waters as defined by the 1920 treaty.[5]

These agreements were superseded by the Soviet-Finnish peace treaty of March 12, 1940.[6] Finland having lost the war with Russia, the state boundary was modified to the advantage of the Soviet Union. All of the boundaries of both Finnish and Soviet territorial waters provided for in the pre-1940 agreements were now within the boundaries of the USSR. A protocol to the peace treaty, signed April 29, 1940, listed the boundaries of Soviet and Finnish territorial waters and provided for a three and a half-mile wide passage at the northern extremity of Sursari Island to enable free navigation to the north. A Soviet-Finnish commercial treaty of June 28, 1940, gave most-favored-nation treatment to vessels, passengers, and cargo in territorial waters, and on October 11, 1940, an agreement established a three-mile territorial water belt around the demilitarized Aaland Islands.[7] These provisions were affirmed in the Soviet-Finnish peace treaty of February 10, 1947. Pursuant to that document, the breadth of Soviet territorial waters in the Gulf of Finland became twelve miles, except around Sursari Island.[8]

A Soviet-Finnish agreement which entered into force on May 25, 1966, modified the boundary somewhat in the Gulf of Finland. The coordinates were set forth more precisely, and the contracting parties agreed not to extend their territorial waters in the Gulf of Finland to the west of Sursari Island nor their fishing and other zones beyond certain specified geographic coordinates.[9]

A protocol of March 18, 1958, between the Soviet Union and Poland delimited Soviet territorial waters in the Gulf of Gdansk. The boundary follows a line perpendicular to the shoreline at the terminal point of the Polish-Soviet state boundary on the Baltiiskaia Kosa up to the point of intersection with the outer limit of Polish territorial waters. An extension of this line in the same direction to the point of intersection with the outer limit of Soviet territorial waters constitutes the boundary of Soviet territorial waters.[10]

From 1917 to 1940, the Soviet Union had no shoreline on the Baltic Sea itself. With the incorporation of Latvia, Estonia, and Lithuania into the Soviet Union in 1940, the

USSR acquired extensive jurisdiction over Baltic coastlines. Prior to 1940, the Baltic states had applied the three-mile rule except for customs jurisdiction. Latvia and Estonia had re-enacted the 1909 customs law of the Russian empire providing for a twelve-mile customs zone.

Following World War II, Soviet enforcement of its twelve-mile claim in the Baltic resulted in the seizure of more than fifty Danish fishing vessels and numerous Swedish vessels. An exchange of diplomatic protests occurred, but not until May 26, 1950, did the Soviet Union acknowledge that its legal claim was predicated on the 1927 statute on the state boundary. The Scandinavian countries asserted that territorial waters were limited to a maximum of four miles by Baltic custom. The Soviet Union replied that there were no generally recognized norms of international law with respect to the breadth of territorial waters. Enforcement of the Soviet claim has continued, and it is noteworthy that incidents have occurred even while the Soviet Union has been assiduously cultivating better relations with Scandinavia. [11]

It has been argued that the Soviet claim to a twelve-mile belt of territorial waters in the Baltic Sea is invalid because the Soviet legislation invoked to support the claim was adopted before Baltic waters washed Soviet coasts. According to this view, sovereignty over territorial waters is a series of rights appurtenant to the mainland. By the law of state succession, the Soviet Union acquired only those rights exercised by Estonia, Latvia, and Lithuania; i.e., a three-mile limit. [12]

However, presumably before their incorporation into the Soviet Union the Baltic states could themselves have extended the limits of their territorial waters to twelve miles, and after their incorporation the Soviet Union could have specifically done so by statute. Thus, the question is reduced to whether all-union legislation in force when the Baltic states were admitted automatically applied retroactively and superseded contrary practices of those states prior to their annexation. The statute in question is the 1927 statute on the state boundary, an all-union law enacted under the authority of Article 14(i) of the USSR Constitution, which vests jurisdiction over state security to the exclusive competence of the Union. It could be argued that the all-union legislation, in the absence of a specific proviso otherwise, applied only prospectively to the Baltic states. But the republics were admitted to the Union in 1940 as equals with other union republics, which meant that they enjoyed all the rights and privileges of a union republic, including those laws in force prior to incorporation that defined the competence of the union republics. Thus, Soviet boundary regulations as prescribed in the 1927 statute automatically extended to the Baltic coasts when the Baltic republics entered the Union. Whether the 1927 statute actually established a twelve-mile breadth of territorial waters is another question.

The Soviet Union, according to some Soviet jurists, is justified in claiming the Riga Bay as a historic bay incorporated into Russian territory by the Treaty of Nystad of 1721.[13]

The assertion of Molodtsov and others that the Baltic Sea is a closed sea has had no tangible impact on the regime of Soviet territorial waters. Soviet media contain articles from time to time protesting the presence or proximity of vessels of the North Atlantic Treaty Organization to the area and urge neutralization of the Baltic in accordance with the regional seas concept.[14]

BLACK SEA

Geographically, the Black Sea is noteworthy for its smooth coastline, for the absence of river deltas (excluding the Danube), and for the small number of islands in the Sea. It is connected with the Mediterranean Sea and the world's important maritime routes by straits, whose regime is administered by Turkey under the 1936 Montreux Convention.

The Black Sea has enormous economic significance to the Soviet Union as the most important and relatively ice-free artery to world markets. The Sea is a major cabotage route connecting the industrial and agricultural regions of the southern RSFSR, the Ukraine, and the Caucasus. Eleven ports are listed as being open to foreign vessels.[15]

The regime of Soviet territorial waters does not differ from that of other seas bordering the country.[16] Because of the smooth coastline, the twelve-mile limit is calculated from the normal low water line.[17]

The Soviet Union is party to the Black Sea Fisheries Agreement of June 12, 1959, which provides for a mixed commission to draft proposals regarding proper fishing techniques, protection of marine life, coordination of national economic plans, and economic exploitation of the Black Sea fisheries. Its functions are advisory and technical.[18]

SEA OF AZOV

Located on the southern extremity of the Great Russian Plain, the Sea of Azov is almost enclosed by land. The length of the shoreline is 1,612 miles. The Sea is connected with the Black Sea by the Kerchenskii Strait. Some geographers consider the Sea of Azov to be a bay of the Black Sea.[19] Portions of the Sea freeze during the winter, but ports are kept open by ice-breakers. Azov seaports handle primarily coasting trade.

Most Soviet jurists look upon the Azov as an internal sea.[20] This would imply that the Azov is administered as internal waters of the Soviet Union, although no Soviet author has so stated directly. However, the 1928 regulations on the use of wireless radio equipment by foreign vessels in Soviet waters require a special written permit, the validity of which is limited to each special visit to the Sea of Azov, to be issued by the head of the corresponding commercial port.[21] At present the ports of Zhdanov and Berdiansk are listed as being open to foreign vessels.[22]

CASPIAN SEA

The Caspian Sea is a completely landlocked body of water bordered by the Soviet Union and Iran. The northern portion of the Sea is frozen during the winter months, and navigation must be suspended. Variations in sea depths between the northern and southern portions of the Sea necessitate that vessels sailing to the north not be fully loaded, thereby contributing to substantial underutilization of available maritime transport. The Caspian is an insignificant maritime route in terms of total Soviet cargo turnover. However, the Sea and the mouth of the Volga River are a prime source of valuable fish and caviar.

The legal regime of the Caspian is unique. The Caspian is truly a large lake which historically has been called a sea. General norms of international law relating to the high seas, to vessels and their crews sailing on the high seas, and to research and exploitation of natural resources of the high seas do not extend to the Caspian, whose regime is governed by Soviet-Iranian treaties and agreements.

In a treaty of friendship with Iran signed February 26, 1921, the Government of the RSFSR abrogated all treaties, agreements, and conventions of the Tsarist Government and annulled Russian concession rights in the Caspian.[23] The Soviet Union and Iran have equal rights in navigating the Caspian in vessels under their respective flags. The Iranian Government has agreed to exclude from the Iranian fleet subjects of a third government who would use their presence for unfriendly ends with respect to Russia. The 1921 agreement was affirmed by the nonaggression and neutrality pact of 1927, which enjoined the parties from taking part in "political alliances or agreements directed against the safety of . . . territorial waters. . ."[24] In addition the Iranian Government agreed not to keep non-Iranian subjects, including former subjects of third powers who accepted Iranian nationality, among employees, laborers, and contractors at Port Pehlevi for a period of twenty-five years. The Soviet Union may demand the removal of such persons.

A 1927 fisheries agreement set up a joint Soviet-Iranian Company and granted it special concession privileges to catch and process fish. The concession lasted for twenty-five years. Iran elected not to renew the arrangement in 1953, but is bound not to grant a concession with respect to these fisheries to a third government for an additional twenty-five years.

Merchant vessels of the parties in the Caspian Sea receive national treatment in each other's ports, including the assessment of port fees. Each party has reserved a ten-mile fishing zone contiguous to its shore for vessels under its own flag; outside these zones fishing may be engaged in exclusively by Soviet and Iranian nationals. Other maritime trades are restricted to national waters. The continental shelf and its resources are reserved for each party within its portion of the Sea. Sanitary measures applicable to the vessels of one party while in the ports of the other are regulated by the 1926 International Quarantine Convention.[25]

The regime of the Caspian Sea is not regulated by international legal norms relating to either closed or high seas. Under the 1935 decree on fishing, the Soviet part of the Caspian was deemed to be Soviet internal waters.[26] Soviet flag vessels are governed by internal legislation while engaged in coasting trade, but this legislation is superseded by the 1940 treaty provisions with respect to intercourse between the Soviet Union and Iran. In the latter instance Soviet vessels are governed by the Merchant Shipping Code of the USSR.

The provisions of the 1960 statute on the state boundary apply to the Caspian insofar as the statute regulates border lakes. There are no territorial waters in the Caspian, only the ten-mile fishing zone.[27] The entire Sea is open to fishing vessels of both states except in these zones.

The Soviet-Iranian treaties do not contain provisions affecting the navigation of Soviet or Iranian warships on the Caspian or the flight of aircraft over it. Some Soviet publicists, evidently assuming that the international regime of territorial waters and the Soviet rules relating to visits of foreign warships applied to the Caspian, have written that Soviet and Iranian warships may not cross the state sea boundary without the permission of authorities of the other state.[28] A more recent study suggests that Iranian warships have the right to navigate in the Soviet part of the Caspian and Iranian aircraft to fly over with permission, and *vice versa*. The regime of territorial waters in no way extends to the Caspian.[29] The Sea is closed to all vessels of third states.

In an exchange of notes on September 15, 1962, Iran agreed that it would "not accord to any foreign state the right to have missile bases of any type on the territory of Iran."[30] Soviet jurists have interpreted the notes as barring the creation of foreign missile and naval bases on Iranian territory and the Caspian Sea.[31]

ARAL SEA

The Aral Sea is a completely landlocked body of water whose shoreline extends for some 4,000 miles. It serves as a water transit route between the Kazakh and Uzbek Union Republics and provides water for irrigation to surrounding areas.

In fact, the Aral Sea is a large lake; it is traversed primarily by barges. Maritime navigation is governed solely by Soviet legislation regulating internal water routes of the Soviet Union.[32]

THE FAR EASTERN COAST

The far eastern coast of the Soviet Union is bordered by the Sea of Japan, the Okhotsk Sea, and the Bering Sea. These seas serve as an international maritime route for the Soviet Union, affording an uninterrupted link with all other seas. Seven ports and three roadsteads are open to foreign merchant vessels.[33]

The Sea of Japan is bounded by the shores of the Asian mainland and islands; access to the Sea is gained through numerous straits. This geographic configuration has led Soviet jurists in recent years to describe the Sea of Japan as a closed sea. In the draft USSR peace treaty with Japan, the Soviet Union proposed to close the straits leading into the Sea of Japan to the warships of noncontiguous states.[34] Bitter disputes with Japan over fishing rights have existed since the 1920's, when pursuant to Soviet legislation and treaties Japan received preferential fishing privileges along the far eastern Soviet coast. These treaties lost force after World War II. Territorial waters along far eastern Soviet shores were regulated in accordance with the 1927 statute on the state boundary -- and now by the 1960 statute -- and other legislative acts.[35] Japanese-Soviet relations worsened with the incorporation of Peter the Great Bay into Soviet internal waters, and at various times the Soviet Union has threatened to close portions of the Sea of Japan to Japanese fishermen.

On June 12, 1956, the USSR and the People's Republics of China, Vietnam, and Korea, later joined by Outer Mongolia, signed a convention to organize a program of oceanographic and sea life research in the Western Pacific, including the Sea of Japan, to promote conservation of fisheries in the territorial waters of the parties and elsewhere. A commission has been created to coordinate research in fisheries, oceanography, fresh water liminology, and protection of fishing resources.[36]

The Okhotsk Sea is a broad basin deeply indenting the Asian mainland. It is bounded by Soviet territory on all sides except for the Japanese Island of Hokkaido. As in the Sea of Japan, access is gained through straits. Many Soviet jurists consider the Okhotsk Sea to be both a closed and historic sea and would prohibit the navigation of foreign warships therein.[37] There are no international maritime routes of significance through the Sea.

The Bering Sea is the largest and deepest of those washing Soviet shores. It serves as a maritime route for vessels sailing the Northern Sea Route to Murmansk. Fishing and sealing are important and highly regulated activities in the region.

ARCTIC COAST

The Arctic coastline is divided into sectors, which are termed seas, by groups of islands lying on a broad shelf between the coast and the Arctic Ocean. The shallow Barents Sea borders the Soviet Murmansk coasts, the islands of the Spitzbergen-Franz Josef groups, and Novaia Zemlia.

The southern coast is generally smooth east of the narrow fault-controlled entrance to the White Sea. The Kara Sea lies between Novaia Zemlia and the islands of Severnaia Zemlia. Ice floes frequently jam the straits between the Kara and Laptev Seas, rendering navigation extremely hazardous. Ice formation occurs much more rapidly in the Laptev, East Siberian, and Chukotsk Seas; navigation is normally possible from July to September.[38]

In 1921 the RSFSR extended the twelve-mile fishing zone established by the Tsarist Government for the Maritime Province to the White Sea and Arctic coast. On April 15, 1926, the USSR Central Executive Committee categorically defined the boundaries of the Soviet Arctic:

> The Union of Soviet Socialist Republics proclaims as territories all lands and islands already discovered or discovered in the future which at the time of publication of this decree are not recognized by the Government of the Union of Soviet Socialist Republics as territories of any foreign state and which lie in the Arctic Ocean north of the shores of the Union of Soviet Socialist Republics up to the North Pole between the meridian 32°04'35" E. long. from Greenwich, running along the eastern side of Vaida Bay through the triangular marker on Cape Kekurskii, and the meridian 168°49'30" W. long. from Greenwich, bisecting the strait separating the Ratmanov and Krusenstern Islands of the Diomede group in the Bering Sea.[39]

The decree disturbed some Soviet jurists, for it specified only "lands and islands". E. A. Korovin urged that the intent of the decree was to include the ice blocks and waters washing the lands and islands.[40] Korovin's interpretation of the decree was not widely accepted at the time it was advanced.

Another Soviet jurist, V. L. Lakhtin, subdivided the Arctic seas which were free of ice into categories: (1) the mouths of rivers, bays, and landlocked seas whose aperture is not broader than twice the breadth of the marginal sea, such as the White Sea and Kara Sea, which would be regarded as national waters; (2) territorial waters lying between the islands of archipelagoes; (3) remaining waters, which were analogous to territorial waters. In the latter two categories, sovereignty of the coastal state would be limited by the right of innocent passage, but the rights of police, customs, and sanitary control would be exercised by the Soviet Union.[41] Lakhtin considered the Kara Sea to be a closed sea, landlocked by ice. This implied a shifting criterion for the establishment of territorial boundaries. As the ice shifted, so did the territorial waters. Vessels sailing in the area could pass in and out of Soviet jurisdiction several times a day without altering course. As Lakhtin's theory would not provide the requisite degree of Soviet sovereignty in the zone established by the 1926 decree, it was not generally accepted by other Soviet jurists.

After World War II, the Soviet Union was confronted by a changed situation in the Arctic. The strategic vulnerability of the Northern Sea Route with respect to the transfer of warships from west to east was demonstrated vividly in 1940 when a German auxiliary cruiser made the eastward voyage in fourteen days actual running time. With the developing estrangement between the Soviet Union and the Allies and the gradual withdrawal and isolation of the USSR from the world community, Soviet jurists developed theories to support Soviet claims to exclusive sovereignty over Arctic seas.[42]

S. A. Vyshnepolskii's article in Soviet State and Law was the point of departure for later Soviet writings. His argument may be summarized as follows: The Arctic seas are not open because navigation is not possible in the customary sense of the word. Vessels attempting to navigate require the assistance of special icebreakers and other services from the coastal state; i.e., vessels must be led through the seas. There is no normal international navigation, and there are special risks of being caught in the ice, an occurrence which places special and excessive burdens to render aid on the coastal state.

The Northern Sea Route, he continued, historically is a national route. Russians began to use it in the sixteenth century. The Soviet Union undertakes regular planned voyages annually through these waters, whereas other nations do not. The Laptev, East Siberian, and Chukotsk Seas are seas of the bay type; i.e., bays of the Arctic basin. They are navigated only by Soviet vessels and do not form part of an international maritime route. In the Kara Sea Russia has a special historical tradition. In 1582 the English were granted exclusive trading privileges in the mouths of certain northern rivers by Muscovy. From 1616-1620 the Tsar issued four edicts prohibiting commercial navigation in the Kara Sea, which Ivan IV considered as lying "in our land". The Russian regime of the Kara Sea was not protested for more than three hundred years by foreign states. In taking note of this, F. F. Martens concluded the Kara Sea belonged to Russia by uninterrupted and undisputed custom.[43]

In a later publication Vyshnepolskii amplified his argument concerning the coastal character of the Northern Sea Route. In general, he wrote, coastal routes have been allocated to the national shipping of a given state and foreign vessels are not permitted to use them. Whether a particular route is oceanic, regional, or coastal cannot be determined merely by the oceans and basins through which a route passes. The decisive criteria for placing any route in a defined group are the nature of its usage, the destination of cargo, and the initial and final ports of destination of the vessels. On the basis of these criteria, the route of Leningrad to Vladivostok is a coastal route.[44] Vyshnepolskii included the entire area serviced by the Northern Sea Route, even though "the Northern Sea Route is bounded on the west by the passages between the Kara and Barents Seas and on the east by the Bering Strait."[45] Nevertheless, he acknowledged that the Bering and Barents Seas are open seas by virtue of long established fishing activities on the part of many states.

Although Vyshnepolskii's thesis was generally acceptable to many Soviet publicists, disagreement arose as to whether the Arctic seas should be treated as closed seas, which are open to foreign commercial shipping, or as historic bays, which are part of the internal waters of the coastal state. The 1956 naval international law manual recounted extensive Soviet navigation and exploration in the Arctic. In describing the Northern Sea Route as a natural water route of the Soviet Union, the manual compared it to the route along the Norwegian coast and cited the 1951 decision of the International Court of Justice in the Anglo-Norwegian Fisheries Case. No opinion was ventured as to the de facto legal regime prevailing in the Arctic seas.[46] Shmigelskii traced the sovereign rights of the Soviet Union in the Arctic sector to the enormous and effective economic, organizational, and scientific research activities carried on in the northern Polar Basin, the opening of the Northern Sea Route, the explorations and discoveries in polar seas by Russian navigators and explorers, and the historical traditions based on these facts.[47] Shmigelskii clearly implied full sovereignty over the entire Soviet sector.

Zhudro found international recognition of the Soviet Arctic regime in the fact that all foreign vessels which are under contract to Soviet foreign trade organizations for Arctic sailings must agree to be completely subordinate to all instructions transmitted to them by Soviet state agencies responsible for administering Arctic maritime operations. This includes a report upon arrival in the Kara Sea and a daily report of position thereafter. Zhudro believed a generally recognized international custom has thereby been established. In the remainder of the Soviet Arctic zone the Soviet Union may take any special measures, including the prohibition of foreign warships, in order to insure national security.[48]

The 1966 naval international law manual asserted that by virtue of its unique features the Northern Sea Route is under the complete sovereign authority of the Soviet Union. The Route is administered by the Main Administration of Navigation of the Ministry of the Merchant Marine, which replaced Glavsevmorput, formed on December 17, 1932. Merchant vessels have a right of innocent passage along the Route, but are obliged to use Soviet icebreaker and pilot services while navigating the Vilkitskii and Shokalskii Straits. Special rules also govern certain other portions of the Route, including the approaches to the port of Igarka.[49]

There have been recent indications that the Soviet Union intends to promote expanded usage of the Northern Sea Route by foreign vessels. The distance, for example, between Vladivostok, near the Sea of Japan, and Archangel, in north European Russia, is 8,500 miles shorter via the Northern Sea Route in comparison with the Suez Canal route. If the Suez were closed, the savings in time and expense would be multiplied many times. The introduction of Soviet nuclear-powered icebreakers into the Arctic has increased the annual shipping season from 90-100 to 140-150 days. At a news conference in March 1967, V. G. Bakaev, Minister of the Merchant Marine, announced that foreign vessels would be encouraged to refuel and use the port facilities of the isolated ports scattered along the Arctic route.[50] Japanese shipping firms reportedly are negotiating an agreement to use the Northern Sea Route, and the Soviet Union has opened an office in Murmansk to handle the interests of foreign carriers seeking to navigate the Route.[51]

The majority of straits along the Northern Sea Route are less than twenty-four miles wide and therefore come within Soviet territorial waters. Two other straits, the Laptev Strait and Sannikov Strait, are considered to belong to the Soviet Union by historic prescription.[52] These "have never been used for international navigation, and in view of specific natural conditions and frequent ice jams, the legal status of these straits is sharply distinguished from all other straits being used for international navigation."[53] The Rules relating to visits of foreign warships are considered to extend to these straits and to the Northern Sea Route; foreign warships have no right of passage without previous authorization of the Soviet government.

In the summer of 1965 the United States Coast Guard icebreaker _Northwind_ was ordered not to traverse the Vilkitskii Strait while conducting oceanographic research in the face of Soviet protests to the U.S. Department of State. The Soviet Government protested not on the ground that the Arctic seas are Soviet internal waters, but that the _straits_ connecting the seas are Soviet territorial waters.[54] In view of the fact the icebreaker was under quasi-military command and intended to conduct oceanographic research in the Strait, the Soviet legal position probably was well-founded. However, more fortitude and a greater knowledge of the provisions of relevant Soviet legislation would have enabled American authorities to tailor the _Northwind's_ status and activities so that the legal right clearly would be with the

United States. Unfortunately, the affair was badly handled, and the Northwind was unable to complete its original mission of being the first United States vessel to traverse the Northeast Passage.

Notwithstanding Soviet announcements about "opening" the Northern Sea Route and Soviet theories of closed seas and historic bays, the legal regimè of the Soviet Arctic coastline essentially comprises the general provisions regulating territorial waters along other coasts supplemented by rules dictated by the unusual climatic and geographical conditions. The Soviet Government shows every indication of wanting to assimilate the region into the regime of internal waters, but as a matter of international and municipal law this has not yet been accomplished. Ten ports are listed as being open to foreign merchant vessels.[55]

NOTES

1. Dobrovolskii and Zalogin, Moria SSSR (Seas of the USSR) 54-57, 286 (1965). Unless otherwise noted, geographic data on Soviet coasts is based on this study.

2. IM (1966), no. 11.

3. Peace Treaty Between Russia and Finland, October 14, 1920. 3 Dokumenty 277.

4. These were: (1) RSFSR-Finland Agreement of September 20, 1922 reserving fishing rights in their respective territorial waters exclusively to their own nationals, 19 LNTS 143; (2) RSFSR-Finland Convention of October 21, 1922 providing for reciprocal fishing privileges in territorial waters of specified portions of Arctic coasts, 29 LNTS 197; (3) USSR-Finland Agreement of July 28, 1923, on detention procedures in the Gulf of Finland beyond the limits of territorial waters, 32 LNTS 101; (4) Multipartite Convention of August 19, 1925, on the prevention of smuggling of alcoholic beverages, 42 LNTS 73; (5) USSR-Estonia-Finland Agreement of August 19, 1925, concerning

boundary zones for control of smuggling activities implementing no. 4, 42 LNTS 88; (6) USSR-Finland Customs Convention of April 13, 1929, 96 LNTS 93.

5. SZ SSSR (1930), no. 44, item 450.

6. 10 SDD 11-17.

7. Vedomosti SSSR, September 12, 1940, no. 30; 10 SDD 17-20.

8. 13 SDD 26-54; 48 UNTS 203.

9. Suomen Asetuskokoelman Sopimussarja. Ulkovaltain Kanssa Tehdyt Sopimukset (Series of Agreements of the Collected Statutes of Finland: Agreements with Foreign States) (1966), no. 20.

10. 340 UNTS 94.

11. Schapiro, "The Limits of Russian Territorial Waters in the Baltic," 27 British Yearbook of International Law 440 (1950); Glenn, "The Swedish-Soviet Territorial Sea Controversy in the Baltic," 50 American Journal of International Law 942-949 (1956).

12. Schapiro, ibid. Bouchez shares Schapiro's view. He believes a "successor state cannot extend its sovereignty over a water area which did not fall under the sovereignty of its predecessor." Bouchez, The Regime of Bays in International Law 69 (1964).

13. Levin and Kaliuzhnaia, Mezhdunarodnoe pravo (International Law) 190 (1964).

14. See, for example, Pogodin, "Bonn's Strategic Plans in the Baltic," 1961 International Affairs, no. 9, pp. 33-37.

15. Op. cit. supra note 2.

16. Soviet claims to a closed status have had no ascertainable effect on the legal regime of Soviet territorial waters in the Black Sea.

17. Bakhov, Voenno-morskoi mezhdunarodno-pravovoi spravochnik (Naval International Law Manual) 231 (1956).

18. Grzybowski, The Socialist Commonwealth of Nations 168 (1964).

19. Dobrovolskii and Zalogin, op. cit. supra note 1, at 42.

20. Bakhov, op. cit. supra note 17, at 114.

21. SZ SSSR (1928), no. 48, item 431.

22. Op. cit. supra note 2.

23. 1 SDD 148-153; 9 LNTS 383.

24. 10 Dokumenty 396-402; 112 LNTS 275.

25. 10 SDD 56-71; 144 BFSP 419-431.

26. SZ SSSR (1935), no. 50, item 420. The provisions were confirmed in the 1954 decree on fishing. See Barabolia, Voenno-morskoi mezhdunarodno-pravovoi spravochnik (Naval International Law Manual) 374 (1966).

27. The Bureau of Intelligence and Research of the U.S. Department of State has erroneously asserted that the "margins" of the Caspian Sea are claimed as territorial waters. See U.S. Department of State, Sovereignty of the Sea 16 (Geographic Bull. No. 3 1965).

28. 3 Meshera, Morskoe pravo: pravovoi rezhim morskikh putei (Maritime Law; Legal Regime of Maritime Routes) 11-12 (1959); Bahkov, op. cit. supra note 17. at 258.

29. Barabolia, op. cit. supra note 26, at 375.

30. Ibid. at 383-384.

31. Ibid. at 375.

32. Article 4, Ustav vnutrennogo vodnogo transporta SSSR (Charter of Inland Water Transport of the USSR).

33. Op. cit. supra note 2.

34. Pravda, September 7, 1951.

35. See Nikolaev, Problema territorialnykh vod v mezhdunarodnom prave (Problem of Territorial Waters in International Law) 194 (1954).

36. Mikhailov, "Mezhdunarodno-pravovoe regulirovanie rybolovstva i drugikh promyslov na tikhom okeane," (International Legal Regulation of Fishing and Other Maritime Trades in the Pacific Ocean) 1960 Sovetskii ezhegodnik mezhdunarodnogo prava (Soviet Yearbook of International Law) 192-193 (1961).

37. Bakhov, op. cit. supra note 17, at 55; Kozhevnikov, Kurs mezhdunarodnogo prava (Textbook of International Law) 213-214 (2d ed. 1966), citing an 1853 Instruction of the Tsarist Government.

38. Mellor, Geography of the U.S.S.R. 45-46 (1964). Also see Taracouzio, Soviets in the Arctic (1938); Armstrong, The Northern Sea Route: Soviet Exploitation of the North East Passage (1952); Krypton, The Northern Sea Route and the Economy of the Soviet North (1956).

39. Izvestia, April 16, 1926. Also see Zinger, Osnovnye zakony po krainemu severu: pravo na poliarnye prostranstva i organizatsiia organov upravleniia (Basic Laws Concerning the Far North: Law on Polar Expanses and Organizations of Agencies of Administration) 71-72 (1935).

40. Korovin, "SSSR i poliarnye zemli," (The USSR and Polar Lands) 1926 Sovetskoe pravo (Soviet Law), no. 3, p. 46.

41. Lakhtin, "Rights Over the Arctic," 24 American Journal of International Law 703-717 (1930).

42. Expansive claims to sovereignty over northern seas by no means have been confined to Russia. In his Mare Clausum, John Selden concluded that "the very shores or ports of the neighbor-princes beyond sea, are bounds of the sea-territorie of the British Empire, to the southward

and eastward; but that in the open and vast ocean of the north and west, they are to be placed at the utmost extent of those most spacious seas, which are possest by the English, Scots, and Irish." Nedham, Of the dominion, or ownership of the sea 459 (1652).

43. Vyshnepolskii, "K probleme pravovogo rezhim arkticheskoi oblasti," (On the Problem of the Legal Regime of Arctic Regions) 1952 Sovetskoe gosudarstvo i pravo (Soviet State and Law), no. 7, pp. 36-45.

44. Vyshnepolskii, Mirovye morskie puti i sudokhodstvo (World Maritime Routes and Navigation) 52-53 (1953).

45. Krypton, op. cit. supra note 38, at 22.

46. Bakhov, op. cit. supra note 17, at 188.

47. Shmigelskii and Iasinovskii, Osnovy sovetskogo morskogo prava (Fundamental Principles of Soviet Maritime Law) 42 (1963).

48. Zhudro, et. al., Morskoe pravo (Maritime Law) 100 (1964).

49. Barabolia, op. cit. supra note 26, at 288-289.

50. The New York Times, March 29, 1967.

51. The New York Times, June 13, 1967.

52. Barabolia, op. cit. supra note 26, at 289.

53. Ibid.

54. For an account of the voyage made in 1965 and the concomitant exchange of diplomatic correspondence see the Boston Globe, August 29, 1965, p. 22; The New York Times, August 19, 1965; October 17, 1965; summarized in Butler, "Soviet Concepts of Innocent Passage," 7 Harvard International Law Journal 113-114 (1965). A full account of the voyage is chronicled in Petrow, Across the Top of Russia (1967).

55. Op. cit. supra note 2.

CHAPTER 9 PERSPECTIVES

The developing legal regime of Soviet territorial waters in theory and state practice has been the product of historical tradition, national security requirements, economic interests in coastal waters, and the exigencies of commercial intercourse with foreign states. Although no single factor can be said to have predominated to the exclusion of others, considerations of national defense and economic sovereignty were of much greater concern after the Second World War than before, and the element of international commerce received correspondingly less weight.

In the first thirty years of Soviet rule, Soviet jurists derived the great majority of their doctrines on maritime law from the West and from their Russian predecessors. Notwithstanding A. N. Nikolaev's attempt to recast prewar Soviet legal history, Soviet international maritime law did not break sharply with the past. The pattern of Soviet fishing legislation clearly was an extension of measures initiated by the Tsarist Government to reserve coastal fisheries for Russian nationals. Other legislative enactments followed a basically traditional pattern. The right of innocent passage was recognized in theory and practice. The exercise of criminal and civil jurisdiction in coastal waters and the application of customs, sanitary, fishing, pilotage, wireless radio usage, and navigation norms were in no way revolutionary contributions to the law of nations. Those publicists who did press the view that territorial waters are a constituent part of the littoral state were in the tradition of Martens and others, and this school of thought was not generally accepted in the Soviet Union until the eve of World War II.

There is legitimate doubt as to whether the Soviet Union had effectively promulgated a twelve-mile breadth for territorial waters prior to 1960. Until 1945, Soviet state practice more closely approximated the traditional exercise of territorial jurisdiction in contiguous zones. As Nikolaev discovered, great inconsistency in terminology pervaded Soviet statutes purporting to regulate "territorial" waters. And, although eight of twenty-two normative acts used the formula "territorial waters", many of these were relatively unimportant, internally inconsistent, repealed, or did not invoke the twelve-mile rule. The most important statute of this period, the 1927 statute on the state boundary, established a maritime belt twelve miles in breadth; it did not use the term territorial waters.[1] Moreover, Article 23 of the 1927 statute referred to "state water boundaries of the USSR as well as the maritime belt (Art. 9(c)) of the high seas which wash the shores of the USSR. . ." The powers accorded to the Soviet border guard within this "maritime belt" were customary police powers.[2] Finally, the 1947 international law textbook did not claim a twelve-mile limit for Soviet territorial waters.[3]

Although most prewar laws regulating maritime questions continued in force until 1960, Soviet state practice and Soviet jurists began to interpret them in the postwar period as establishing a twelve-mile belt of territorial waters under the exclusive sovereignty of the littoral state. The Soviet Government enforced the 1927 statute against Scandinavian vessels in the Baltic as though it had created a twelve-mile limit. Ironically, the Scandinavian states did not cite the statutory language against the Soviet assertion of jurisdiction. The 1960 statute on the state boundary ended all confusion by specifically providing for a twelve-mile belt of territorial waters.

In a recent and authoritative monograph, a prominent Soviet jurist and diplomat, G. I. Tunkin, reminded his readership that the influence of political and legal ideology on various international legal positions of states is unequal. Ideology is more relevant to general theoretical problems. Its influence diminishes on concrete questions of international law which do not affect the major interests of states.[4] Several pages later Tunkin referred to the 1958 Geneva Conference on the Law of the Sea as an example of divergent "socialist" and "bourgeois" conceptions of international law. The questions of the breadth of territorial waters, the innocent passage of foreign warships, and the immunity of state merchant vessels from coastal jurisdiction could not be resolved in the final Convention,

Tunkin wrote, because of sharp divergencies between the two conceptions of international law; i.e., basic ideological differences.[5]

An analysis of the Soviet regime of territorial waters and of the proceedings at the 1958 and 1960 Geneva conferences suggests that Tunkin's evaluation is highly oversimplified. Soviet efforts to obtain recognition of the twelve-mile limit for territorial waters as a rule of international law enjoyed the influential support of many other states, principally the smaller emerging countries. Indeed, in 1967 a majority of littoral states have adopted the twelve-mile limit for a variety of reasons, primarily security and economic, which bear no relationship to socialism or socialist principles of law. Similarly, many states required previous notification or authorization for visits by foreign warships to territorial waters before the Soviet Union did so by law in 1960. Rather than divergent "conceptions" of international law, it would be more accurate to attribute the differences among states at the Geneva conferences to varying perceptions of their national interests depending upon the particular issue under discussion.

The Soviet preoccupation with strategic and economic considerations, and to some degree Soviet ideological predispositions, are reflected more in the doctrines of closed seas and historic bays and a tendency to resort to unilateral characterization of the legality of Soviet actions than in the proceedings at Geneva. The twelve-mile rule is apparently regarded as only a first line of defense. To further minimize the influence over and accessibility of other powers to Soviet coasts, Soviet jurists have elaborated the closed sea and historic bay doctrines. The former, in the opinion of most Soviet publicists, applies to six of fourteen seas washing the Soviet Union. The latter applies to the four Arctic seas. The Caspian and Aral Seas occupy a special status. Thus, only the Barents and Bering Seas are regarded as open seas.

In legal terms a persuasive case can be made for the Soviet viewpoint. The closed seas do not contain major international shipping routes, and they would remain open to the commercial shipping of all states. The Arctic seas originally were explored by Russians and have been effectively and extensively developed by the Soviet Union.

The principal legal difficulty with the Soviet positions is that Soviet jurists do not consider the general applicability of these principles to other bodies of water in the world and their consequences for international trade and regional peace. For where international convention and custom have long served to quiet maritime disputes, the Soviet theories would introduce conflict and chaos. In a world community where a balance must be maintained between legitimate security needs of the coastal state and the requirements of international commerce, many of the Soviet claims, particularly those relating to historic bays and seas, are extreme or unfounded; these are likely to continue to be subordinated to broader maritime interests in freedom of navigation.

NOTES

1. SZ SSSR (1927), no. 62, item 625.

2. Ibid., Articles 25 and 26.

3. Durdenevskii and Krylov, Mezhdunarodnoe pravo (International Law) 252-254 (1947).

4. Tunkin, Ideologicheskaia borba i mezhdunarodnoe pravo (Ideological Struggle and International Law) 17-18 (1967).

5. Ibid. at 36-38.

DOCUMENTARY APPENDIXES

A LEGISLATION

Appendix 1

ON THE PROCLAMATION OF LANDS AND ISLANDS LOCATED IN THE NORTHERN ARCTIC OCEAN AS TERRITORY OF THE USSR

Decree of the Presidium of the Central Executive Committee of the USSR, April 16, 1926. SZ SSSR (1926), no. 32, item 203.

The Presidium of the Central Executive Committee of the USSR decrees:

All lands and islands, both discovered and which may be discovered in the future, which do not comprise at the time of publication of the present decree the territory of any foreign state recognized by the Government of the USSR, located in the Northern Arctic Ocean, north of the shores of the Union of Soviet Socialist Republics up to the North Pole between the meridian 32° 04'35" E. long. from Greenwich, running along the eastern side of Vaida Bay through the triangular marker on Cape Kekurskii, and the meridian 168°49'30" W. long. from Greenwich, bisecting the strait separating the Ratmanov and Krusenstern Islands of the Diomede group in the Bering Sea, are proclaimed to be territory of the USSR.

Appendix 2

ON USE OF WIRELESS RADIO TRANSMISSION EQUIPMENT BY FOREIGN VESSELS WHILE IN WATERS OF THE USSR

Decree of the Council of People's Commissars of the USSR, July 24, 1928. SZ SSSR (1928), no. 48, item 431.

(Excerpt)

Article 1. The use of a vessel's wireless radio transmission equipment by foreign warships and nonmilitary vessels situated within the limits of the maritime border belt of the

USSR or in the internal waters of the USSR within a distance of ten miles from shore shall be permitted only on the grounds set forth in the present decree.

Article 2. Any exchange of radiograms shall be prohibited for nonmilitary foreign vessels situated in districts where shore radio stations are located, except in instances specified in Article 7 of the present decree.

Article 3. The use of a vessel's wireless radio transmission equipment may be granted to nonmilitary foreign vessels situated in those ports from which the nearest shore radio station is at a distance of more than ten miles radius, as well as within the limits of the Sea of Azov, only by a special written permit issued by the head of the appropriate commercial port for a period or for each individual instance of a visit by the vessel to the ports and internal waters of the USSR.

In instances where the nearest shore radio station belonging to the People's Commissariat for Military and Maritime Affairs or other department is located at a distance of not more than ten miles radius from the corresponding commercial port, the aforementioned foreign vessels shall receive permission for a radio exchange from the head of the commercial port only by agreement with the local representatives of the appropriate departments.

Article 4. The local command of naval forces shall be granted the right to restrict a radio exchange of foreign warships situated within the limits of the ten mile belt, with respect both to the duration of conversations and to the districts in which they are conducted, and also with respect to the wave length.

Article 5. The head of the nearest commercial port shall see to it that the rules of Article 2 of the present decree are enforced.

He shall close and seal the wireless radio transmission equipment of nonmilitary foreign vessels throughout the entire stay of such vessels in port or their anchorage within the limits of the ten-mile belt specified in Article 1 of the present decree.

Article 6. Foreign vessels standing at anchor in quarantine and having need for radio communications with a local shore radio-station may, in exceptional instances, use a radio receiver with minimum power or the vessel's wireless radio transmission equipment with slight power, on days and hours notified by the said station.

Article 7. Restrictions on the right to use a vessel's wireless radio transmission equipment provided for by Articles 2-6 of the present decree shall not extend: a) to a vessel which is in danger or which transmits a communication in order to avert an accident; b) to a vessel rendering assistance to another vessel in distress; and c) the conducting of a vessel through ice.

Upon entry into a port where there are radio stations, foreign vessels shall be permitted, in especially important instances, to finish radio exchanges begun with the corresponding port, but only on the condition that the equipment is transferred to minimum power or to slight power.

Article 8. In all instances of use of a vessel's wireless radio transmission equipment in accordance with the present decree, foreign warships and nonmilitary vessels shall be guided by the pertinent rules of international radio communications adopted by the USSR, as well as by the rules regulating internal radio communication of the USSR. Rules of internal radio communication not announced for general information shall be communicated to foreign vessels upon their arrival in ports of the USSR by appropriate local naval or port authorities.

Article 9. Radio communications of foreign warships and nonmilitary vessels may only be open, without the use of any kind of ciphers or codes, except for the specially designated signals of the international service regulation for radio communications, as well as of the international signal code.

Article 10. The commander or master of an interested foreign vessel shall be considered a person empowered to deal with agencies of authority concerning all questions deriving from the present decree.

Article 11. The rules set forth in the present decree shall retain force only in the event the USSR is not in a state of war, and only with respect to vessels sailing under the flag of non-belligerent states.

Article 12. Persons who have violated the rules set forth in the present decree shall bear responsibility according to the criminal legislation of the appropriate union republics.

Appendix 3

MARITIME SHIPPING CODE OF THE USSR ANNEX V: ON STATE MARITIME PILOTS

June 14, 1929. SZ SSSR (1929), no. 41, item 365, as amended to July 1, 1958.

(Excerpt)

I. Organization of the Pilotage Service

Article 1. The conducting of vessels on the approaches to commercial seaports of the USSR and within the limits of waters of such ports shall be carried out exclusively by state maritime pilots.

Pilotage districts, both obligatory and non-obligatory, shall be established by the People's Commissariat of Water Transport* and shall be published in *Izveshcheniia moreplavateliam.* (Notices to Mariners)

Article 2. Persons who possess a deck officer's certificate not lower than master of short-distance navigation and, in addition, have passed the examination for a pilot's certificate in the specific district may be enrolled as state maritime pilots.

The rules and procedure of examination shall be established by the People's Commissariat of Water Transport.

---

* Since 1946, the Ministry of the Navy.

Article 3. State maritime pilots shall be subordinate to the master of the corresponding ports.

. . .

Article 7. The state shall be responsible for damage caused by the fault of state maritime pilots; however, such responsibility shall be limited by the amounts of the average fund of the given port, formed from 10 per cent deducted from amounts of pilotage fees.

A suit for compensation of losses in such instances may be brought exclusively in judicial and arbitrazh agencies of the USSR and union republics, as appropriate, against the master of the port to whom the pilot is subordinate.

II. Duties of State Maritime Pilots

Article 8. State maritime pilots shall fulfill the following duties:

a) carry out the conducting of vessels (Art. 1);
b) participate in sounding operations;
c) observe the condition and correctness of channel barriers;
d) see to it, during the conducting of the vessel that photographs are not taken of the passage locality and that no sounding is made with devices other than the hand lead;
e) see to it, during the conducting of the vessel, that ballast and coral dust is not thrown into the channels, roadsteads, and harbors.

Article 9. In the event that a vessel has an accident in the district of pilotage service, pilots of the given district must render the vessel all assistance within their power.

. . .

Appendix 4

MARITIME SHIPPING CODE OF THE USSR ANNEX IX: SUNKEN PROPERTY

June 14, 1929. SZ SSSR (1929), no. 41, item 365, as amended to July 1, 1958.

Article 1. The raising of property (vessels, debris of a vessel, objects of vessel's supply, cargo, etc.) which has sunk within the limits of the port waters of the coastal maritime belt, indicated in subsection "c" of Article 9 of the Statute on the Protection of the State Boundary of the USSR, June 15, 1927, (SZ SSSR (1927), no. 62, item 625), or within internal seas of the USSR, shall be carried out on the principles indicated in the following articles.

Article 2. In those instances when property which has sunk within the limits of port waters, channels, or near the borders of a merchant seaport, hinders navigation or the conduct of hydrotechnical work, the Administration of the appropriate merchant port may establish a time period, according to the circumstances of the case, sufficient for the raising of the property, designating a special period for the owner of the property to declare his intention to raise it. If the owner of the sunken property is unknown, the Administration of the port shall place in Izvestiia sovetov deputatov trudiashchikhsia SSSR a single announcement requesting the owner to declare an intention to raise the property and to carry out the raising in the period designated by the Administration of the port.

If the owner of a sunken foreign vessel is unknown, but the flag of such vessel is known, then, in addition to the announcement, the People's Commissariat of Foreign Affairs shall be informed of the designated periods.

Article 3. In those instances when the owner of sunken property indicated in Article 2 does not make a declaration within the designated period to the Administration of the appropriate port of his intention to raise the property, or does not carry out the raising, the Administration of the port shall take measures to raise it, or, if necessary, to destroy or to remove such property by other means.

Article 4. In instances not provided for by Article 2, the owner of sunken property may, within one year from the day when the property was sunk, submit to the appropriate agency of border protection of the USSR a declaration of intention to raise such property. The period in which it is proposed to finish the raising operation must be specified in the declaration. The agency of border protection shall be obliged to designate for the owner a sufficient period for the raising according to the circumstances of the case.

Note. In the event of the sinking of property of the People's Commissariat of Military and Naval Affairs, other than vessels (Article 12), the question of raising such property and of periods for the raising shall be decided by agreement between the People's Commissariats of Military and Naval Affairs and of Border Protection.

Article 5. If property has sunk within waters of sea fortifications and fortified districts, then, irrespective of observance of the rules of Articles 2-4, the permission of the People's Commissariat of Military and Naval Affairs shall be necessary in order to raise such property.

Article 6. The procedure for carrying out the work of raising sunken property, in particular whether permission shall be granted to the owner of such property or to a salvage enterprise designated by him, shall be determined by the appropriate agency of border protection.

Article 7. The owner of sunken property shall lose his rights thereto:

a) when a special period for declaring an intention to raise the sunken property has been given to him (Article 2): from the moment of refusal to raise the property or, if he has not made a direct declaration of refusal, from the moment of expiry of the period, or from the moment of expiry of the period designated to him for raising sunken property, if at such moment the property has not been raised;

b) in the event provided for by Article 4, from the moment

of expiration of a one-year period for declaring an intention to raise the sunken property or of the period designated for raising the property, if this has not been done.

Article 8. In the event of the immediate removal of sunken property which presents a direct danger for navigation, the actions specified in Article 3 may be performed by the Administration of the port and without designating to the owner of the property the periods indicated in Article 2, but with notification of the owner concerning measures taken, if he is known, or with corresponding announcement in Izvestiia sovetov deputatov trudiashchikhsia SSSR, if the owner is unknown.

Measures provided for by the present Article with respect to military property must be previously agreed upon with the People's Commissariat of Military and Naval Affairs.

Article 9. Property raised by the Administration of the port in accordance with Article 8, and, in the event of impossibility or impracticability of preserving it, amounts derived from its sale, shall be given to the owner of the sunken property upon his appearance, if this occurs not later than two years from the day when the property was sunk. Upon the expiry of this period, the owner shall lose his rights to the property.

Article 10. The Administration of a merchant port shall be compensated out of the value of the raised property for expenses connected with the raising of property in accordance with Articles 3 and 8.

Article 11. In those instances when sunken property is raised accidentally, the person who raised it shall be obliged to surrender it to the Administration of the appropriate port, and such person shall have the right to receive an award in the amount of one-third of the value of the raised property.

Article 12. The present Annex (IX) to the Maritime Shipping Code of the USSR shall not extend to naval vessels of the USSR.

Appendix 5

ON SANITARY PROTECTION OF THE BORDERS OF THE USSR

Decree of August 23, 1931. SZ SSSR (1931), no. 55, item 355.

In connection with the ratification by the Government of the USSR of the International Sanitary Convention signed in Paris on June 21, 1926 (SZ SSSR (1929), II, no. 19, item 106), the Central Executive Committee and Council of People's Commissars of the USSR decree:

Article 1. Sanitary protection of the land and sea boundaries of the USSR shall have the purpose of preventing the carrying of contagious diseases from abroad into the USSR and from the USSR abroad.

The following shall be considered to be contagious diseases within the meaning of the present decree: plague, cholera, yellow fever, and also, in the event of an epidemic, typhus and smallpox.

Article 2. Sanitary-medical and sanitary-administrative measures shall be applied for sanitary protection of the boundaries of the USSR.

The following shall be regarded as sanitary-medical measures: separation and isolation of sick persons and those suspected of being sick according to their state of health, bacteriological research, doctor's examination, medical observation, observation, sanitary inspection of freight, baggage, and means of transport, disinfection, extermination of insects and rats, etc.

The following shall be regarded as sanitary-administrative measures: prohibiting entry and exit to individual persons, prohibiting importation or exportation of freight and baggage, closing of individual localities for entry and exit, closing of borders, etc.

Article 3. The closing of individual localities for entry and exit and the closing of land borders shall be conducted by order by the Chief Administration of Border Protection of the Unified State Political Administration in agreement with the People's Commissariats of Health of the union republics and other interested departments.

Other measures concerning sanitary protection of boundaries shall be conducted by health agencies.

Article 4. The instances, procedure, and limits of application of each of the measures indicated in Article 2 shall be established by rules published in elaboration of the present decree observing the International Sanitary Convention of June 21, 1926, and of international sanitary agreements of the USSR with individual states.

These rules shall be published by the People's Commissariats of Health of union republics in agreement with the People's Commissariat of Foreign Affairs, the Unified State Political Administration, the People's Commissariat of Communications, the People's Commissariat of Water Transport, the People's Commissariat of Foreign Trade of the USSR, the All-Union Office of Border Sanitary Information, and the All-Union Unified Civil Air Fleet.

Article 5. With respect to states which are not participants in the International Sanitary Convention of June 21, 1926, and which do not have individual sanitary agreements with the USSR, a different sanitary regime may be established -- which deviates from the rules specified in Article 4 -- if such states apply a sanitary regime to the USSR which contravenes the International Sanitary Convention of June 21, 1926. Such deviations shall be established in the same manner in which the rules specified in Article 4 are published.

Article 6. All citizens and agencies within the USSR shall be obliged to accurately fulfill the requirements of the rules indicated in Article 4 and the orders of agencies carrying out the sanitary protection of the boundaries, based on them.

Violators of such rules and orders shall be subject to judicial responsibility according to the criminal codes of the union republics, or to a fine in an administrative proceeding in an amount up to 100 rubles.

Instances when violators shall be subject to a fine in an administrative proceeding, and the amounts of the fine for individual violations, shall be established by the rules indicated in Article 4.

Fines shall be exacted in the generally-established uncontestable administrative procedure.

Article 7. Notification of foreign states concerning the sanitary condition of the USSR and of the USSR concerning the sanitary condition of foreign states shall be carried out through an All-Union Office of Border Sanitary Information. This Office shall act according to a Statute concerning it, issued by the Council of People's Commissars of the USSR.

Article 8. The rules specified in Article 4 shall establish for what actions of a sanitary-medical character payment may be exacted and the amounts of such payment.

Article 9. Special rules concerning measures of struggle against carrying from abroad into the USSR, and from the USSR abroad, other contagious diseases, in addition to those enumerated in Article 1, may be published in the same manner as those specified in Article 4.

Article 10. The sanitary regime of warships and vessels equivalent thereto shall be established by a special law.

Article 11. The Council of People's Commissars of the USSR shall be charged with introducing changes deriving from the present decree into the legislation of the USSR.

Appendix 6

ON CONSERVATION OF FISHERY RESOURCES AND THE REGULATION OF FISHING IN THE WATERS OF THE USSR

Decree of the Council of Ministers of the USSR, August 10, 1954. United Nations, Laws and Regulations on the Regime of the Territorial Sea (1957).

(Excerpt)

. . .

Article 6. Foreign citizens and juridical persons of foreign states may not engage in commercial fishing or the commercial catching or gathering of other aquatic animals or plants in the waters of the USSR, except as provided for in international agreements concluded by the USSR with foreign states.

. . .

Appendix 7

DECREE OF THE USSR COUNCIL OF MINISTERS REGARDING PETER THE GREAT BAY

Izvestia, July 21, 1957, p. 1.

The Council of Ministers of the USSR has considered the question of the boundaries of Soviet internal waters in the area of Peter the Great Bay and has established that the boundaries of Soviet internal waters in this area and the baseline for calculation seaward of the breadth of Soviet territorial waters shall be the line connecting the mouth of the Tiumen-Ula River with Cape Povorotnyi.

The navigation of foreign vessels, as well as flights of foreign aircraft, in the area of Peter the Great Bay may take place only with the authorization of competent authorities of the USSR, except for instances of entry of foreign vessels to the open port of Nakhodka and departure therefrom. Navigation of foreign vessels to the open port of Nakhodka must be carried out along the channel announced in Notices to Mariners.

Appendix 8

ON THE REPRODUCTION AND ON THE CONSERVATION OF FISHERY RESOURCES IN INTERNAL WATERS OF THE USSR

Decree of the Council of Ministers of the USSR, 1958. SP SSSR, no. 16, item 127 (1958).

(Excerpt)

. . .

7. Foreign citizens and juridical persons of foreign states are forbidden to engage in commercial catching and gathering of fish and other aquatic animals and plants in the waters of the USSR except as provided for in agreements concluded by the USSR with other states.

8. In the catching and gathering of fish and other aquatic animals and plants for industrial purposes and for personal consumption in border waters of the USSR, the rules relating to the border regime must be observed.

. . .

Appendix 9

FUNDAMENTAL PRINCIPLES OF CRIMINAL LEGISLATION OF THE USSR AND UNION REPUBLICS

December 25, 1958. Vedomosti SSSR (1959), no. 1, item 6.

(Excerpt)

. . .

Article 4. Operation of criminal laws of USSR and union republics with respect to acts committed on territory of USSR.

All persons who commit crimes on the territory of the USSR shall be subject to responsibility in accordance with criminal laws in force at the place of commission of the crime.

The question of criminal responsibility of diplomatic representatives of foreign states and other (foreign) citizens who, in accordance with prevailing laws and international agreements, are not subject to criminal jurisdiction in Soviet criminal institutions, in the event of commission of a crime on the territory of the USSR by such persons, shall be decided through diplomatic channels.

Article 5. Operation of criminal laws of USSR and union republics with respect to acts committed outside boundaries of USSR.

Citizens of the USSR who commit crimes abroad shall be subject to criminal responsibility in accordance with the criminal laws prevailing in the union republic on whose territory they are brought to trial or criminal proceedings are instituted.

Stateless persons who are situated in the USSR and who have committed crimes beyond the boundaries of the USSR shall bear responsibility on the same basis.

If the said persons have undergone punishment abroad for the crimes committed, a court may mitigate the assigned punishment accordingly or may completely relieve the guilty person from serving the punishment.

Foreigners shall be subject to responsibility for crimes committed outside the boundaries of the USSR in accordance with Soviet criminal laws in instances provided for by international agreements.

. . .

Appendix 10

STATUTE ON THE PROTECTION OF THE STATE BOUNDARY OF THE UNION OF SOVIET SOCIALIST REPUBLICS

August 5, 1960. Vedomosti SSSR (1960), no. 34, item 324.

I. General Provisions

Article 1. The state boundary of the USSR is the line which determines the land and water territory of the USSR. The perpendicular surface passing along this line is the boundary of airspace and minerals of the USSR.

Article 2. The state boundary of the USSR shall be determined by decisions of the highest agencies of state authority of the USSR and by prevailing agreements of the USSR with other states.

State boundary crossings in localities shall be established by protocol-descriptions and other demarcation documents.

Article 3. Coastal sea waters, 12 nautical miles in breadth, computed from the line of lowest ebb-tide both on the mainland and also around islands, or from the line of the farthest extremity of internal sea waters of the USSR, shall constitute the territorial waters of the USSR. In individual instances provided for by agreements of the USSR with other states, the breadth of territorial waters may be otherwise.

The line of the farthest extremity of territorial waters shall constitute the state boundary of the USSR at sea.

In sections where the territorial waters of the USSR adjoin the territorial waters of neighboring states, the state sea boundary of the USSR shall be established in accordance with agreements concluded by the USSR with adjoining states, or, in the absence of such agreements, in accordance with principles accepted in the international practice of states or by a straight line connecting the headlands of the land boundary to the sea.

Article 4. Internal sea waters of the USSR shall include:

a) waters of ports of the USSR, delimited seaward by lines passing through the farthest extending points of hydrotechnical or other structures of ports seaward;

b) waters of bays, inlets, coves, and estuaries, whose entire shores belong to the USSR, up to a straight line drawn from shore to shore in a place where, seaward, one or several passages are first formed, if the breadth of each of these does not exceed 24 nautical miles;

c) waters of bays, inlets, coves, and estuaries, seas, and straits, historically belonging to the USSR.

Article 5. On navigable border rivers the state boundary of the USSR shall be established along the middle of the main channel or thalweg of a river, and on non-navigable rivers, along the middle of the river or along the middle of the main branch; on border lakes, along the middle of the lake or along a straight line connecting the outlets of the land boundary to the shore of the lake. The state boundary passing through a river or lake shall not be moved either in the event of changes in the outline of the shores or in the level of water or in the event of deviation of the riverbed to one side or the other, unless otherwise provided by agreements of the USSR with other states.

<u>Article 6</u>. The state boundary of the USSR shall be clearly marked by visible boundary markers (boundary posts, pyramids, mounds, flares, buoys, distance markers, and others).

The line of farthest extremity of territorial waters of the USSR in specific places may be marked by buoys and spar-buoys for orientation.

II. Regime of the State Boundary

<u>Article 7</u>. The regime of the state boundary (procedure for movement across the boundary, content of boundary markers, conduct of work on the boundary, etc.) shall be established by legislation of the USSR and by agreements of the USSR with adjoining states.

<u>Article 8</u>. In the interests of protecting the state boundary of the land and water territory of the USSR, a boundary zone and boundary belt shall be established in necessary instances by the Council of Ministers of the USSR or, under its authorization, by the Councils of Ministers of the union republics.

The boundary zone shall be established, as a rule, within the limits of territory of the district, city, rural, or village soviet of working people's deputies which is adjacent to the state boundary. The territorial and internal sea waters of the USSR and the Soviet part of waters of border rivers and lakes shall be included as an organic part of a boundary zone, where such is established. A corresponding regime shall be in effect in the boundary zone.

The breadth of a boundary zone must not exceed two kilometers from the line of the state boundary on land or from the shores of border rivers (or lakes). Within the limits of this belt additional regime restrictions shall be introduced by the border guard.

The Soviet part of waters of border rivers and lakes, and also islands on these rivers and lakes which belong to the USSR, shall be situated under the exclusive control of the border guard.

<u>Article 9</u>. Districts in which the navigation or anchoring of vessels and maritime trade is temporarily or permanently

prohibited may be established by decision of competent agencies in individual sections of the internal sea and territorial waters of the USSR. The establishment of such districts shall be announced in Notices to Mariners.

Article 10. Entry into a boundary zone by persons who are not permanent residents of such zone shall be forbidden without the permission of police agencies, unless a different procedure has been established.

Entry into a boundary belt and residence therein shall be permitted only with the permission of the border guard.

Article 11. Admission of persons across the state boundary of the USSR shall be permitted only if there exist the established formal documents, in the proper form, for the right of entry into the USSR or exit from the USSR, and shall be carried out in places where admission-control points (KPP) of the border guard are located.

Control over conveyance of manuscript materials and printed matter across the boundary shall also be exercised at admission-control points.

Article 12. Admission across the state boundary of the USSR of freight, other property, and valuables, as well as diplomatic mail shall be carried out by customs institutions in accordance with the Customs Code of the USSR and with special instructions.

Agricultural and forestry products, plants, livestock and poultry, as well as products of livestock origin, shall be subject to sanitary-medical, veterinary and phytosanitary control, in addition to customs control.

Article 13. A simplified procedure for admission of persons and of freight crossing with them, other property, and valuables across the state boundary of the USSR may be established by agreement with adjoining states. Such admission may be carried out either at admission-control points or in other places agreed upon with adjoining states.

Article 14. Rail, water, air, motor vehicle, and other communication across the state boundary of the USSR shall be carried out in accordance with prevailing legislation and with agreements of the USSR with other states.

Means of transport, excluding means of air transport, shall be admitted across the boundary at border admission-control points, and aircraft of all types shall cross the boundary in established places (air gateways). The take-off of all aircraft from the territory of the USSR, as well as their landing after crossing the state boundary in flight into the USSR, shall be permitted only at aerodromes where there are admission-control points. A different procedure for flight and landing of aircraft shall be permitted only by special permission of competent agencies.

Article 15. Foreign nonmilitary vessels shall enjoy the right of innocent passage through territorial waters of the USSR. By innocent passage is meant navigation through territorial waters for the purpose of crossing them without entry into internal sea waters or for the purpose of passage into internal sea waters or departure from internal sea waters for the high seas. Passage shall be considered innocent if the vessels follow a customary navigational course or a course recommended by competent agencies, observing the established regime, and in places where there are no districts closed to navigation which have been announced in *Notices to Mariners*.

A list of ports, inlets, and roadsteads open to foreign vessels, the procedure for entry and arrival therein, for carrying out cargo and passenger operations, for communications of vessels with shore, for shore leave for personnel of the vessel's officers and crew, for visits to such vessels by persons who do not belong to the vessel's officers and crew, and other questions connected with the entry of foreign nonmilitary vessels into territorial and internal sea waters of the USSR, shall be regulated by legislation of the USSR and of the union republics, and by special rules and instructions promulgated by competent agencies and published in *Notices to Mariners* and other official publications.

Article 16. Foreign warships shall pass through territorial and enter internal sea waters of the USSR in accordance with the previous authorization of the Government of the USSR in the manner provided for by the rules for visits to territorial and internal sea waters of the USSR by foreign warships, published in Notices to Mariners.

Foreign submarines whose arrival in territorial and internal sea waters of the USSR has been authorized must only navigate on the surface.

Article 17. Foreign warships and nonmilitary vessels, during their stay in territorial and internal sea waters of the USSR, shall be obliged to fulfill navigation, wireless radio, port, customs, sanitary, and other rules established for navigation and stays in such waters.

Article 18. Foreign nonmilitary vessels which have suffered disaster because of being forced not to observe the rules of innocent passage through the territorial waters of the USSR shall be obliged to give notice thereof to the authorities of the nearest Soviet port. The giving of a false signal concerning a disaster for the purpose of illegally entering territorial waters of the USSR or staying in such waters shall be considered a violation of the state boundary of the USSR. Vessels which have given such a signal shall be subject to detention.

Article 19. The conduct of maritime trade (catching of fish, crabbing, killing of marine fur-bearing animals, and any other trade) in the territorial and internal sea waters of the USSR by a foreign vessel shall be prohibited, except in instances when such trade has been authorized by agreement of the USSR with the respective states. Similarly, foreign vessels shall be prohibited from conducting hydrographic work and research in the above-mentioned waters.

Foreign vessels which violate the above-mentioned provisions or, having authorization for maritime trade, conduct it in violation of established rules, shall be subject to detention, and the persons who are guilty thereof shall be brought to responsibility in accordance with legislation of the USSR and of the union republics.

Article 20. Navigation, fishing, cutting of timber, water-usage, and construction of various hydro-installations on border rivers and lakes shall be carried out and regulated on the basis of agreements of the USSR with adjoining states. In the absence of such agreements, navigation, fishing, cutting of timber, and water-usage in the Soviet part of waters of border rivers and lakes shall be permitted on the basis of rules established by competent agencies by agreement with the border guard. The erection of various hydro-installations which do not change the water regime of the river shall be permitted in the same manner.

Article 21. The sending across the state boundary of the USSR of any kind of postal transmissions (letters, printed matter, packages, etc.) shall be carried out with observance of the requirements of the Customs Code of the USSR and in accordance with agreements of the USSR with other states concerning postal exchange.

Article 22. International telephone and telegraph communication across the state boundary of the USSR, inspection and repair of lines of such communication, and also the construction, repair, and use of gas pipelines, oil pipelines, and electro-transmission lines passing across the boundary shall be carried out in accordance with prevailing legislation and agreements of the USSR with other states.

Article 23. Customs, sanitary-medical, veterinary, and phytosanitary control at the state boundary of the USSR shall be carried out by agencies of the Ministry of Foreign Trade, Health, Agriculture, respectively, and at border railroad stations sanitary-medical control shall be exercised by the Ministry of Transportation, on the basis of prevailing legislation and agreements of the USSR with other states. The above-mentioned ministries, by agreement with the border guard, with the Ministry of Foreign Affairs of the USSR, and with other interested departments, shall publish rules, obligatory for all, concerning the carrying out of customs, sanitary-medical, veterinary, and phytosanitary control.

Customs institutions and veterinary and sanitary-quarantine points, which shall be placed at points where the KPP of the border guard are located, shall be organized for carrying out these tasks.

In the event a threat arises of the dissemination of an especially dangerous infection on the territory of the USSR or adjoining state, the boundary at the threatened sections may be temporarily closed by decision of competent agencies, and also a quarantine may be established for people, livestock, freight, and seed, plantings, and other materials.

Article 24. To secure the fulfillment of agreements concerning questions of the regime of the state boundary, of assistance in the fulfillment of other agreements of the USSR with adjoining states concerning boundary questions, and also of the regulation of boundary incidents originating on the state boundary of the USSR, border representatives of the USSR (border commissars, border plenipotentiaries, their deputies and assistants) shall be appointed from among officers of the border guard.

Border representatives of the USSR shall be guided in their work by legislation of the USSR, agreements of the USSR with other states concerning boundary questions, and special instructions.

Questions not regulated by border representatives shall be transmitted for decision by way of diplomacy.

Article 25. In sections of the state boundary of the USSR where there are no specially appointed border representatives, their functions shall be fulfilled by commanders of units of the border guard, acting on the basis of special instructions.

Article 26. The following shall be deemed violators of the state boundary of the USSR:

a) persons who have crossed on foot (or have been conveyed on land or in the air), or who attempt to cross, the state boundary at points not established for crossing the boundary, or, although across established points of crossing, by illegal means;

b) persons who are discovered on means of navigation, or swimming, in territorial and internal sea waters of the USSR, and also in the Soviet part of waters of border rivers and lakes, if they illegally penetrated into such waters or are illegally attempting to leave their limits;

c) foreign warships and nonmilitary vessels which have entered territorial and internal sea waters of the USSR, and also the Soviet part of waters of border rivers and lakes in violation of established rules for entry;

d) aircraft which cross the boundary of airspace of the USSR, if they do not have permission of competent Soviet agencies to fly across the boundary and over the land or water territory of the USSR, and also, even though they have the above-mentioned permission, if they fly across the boundary at a non-established place or in violation of the altitude of the flight.

Article 27. Persons who have violated or who attempt to violate the state boundary of the USSR, and also persons who send or attempt to send across the state boundary of the USSR objects, materials, currency, and negotiable valuables prohibited for import or export, as well as their accomplices, shall be subject to detention and prosecution in accordance with legislation of the USSR and of the union republics.

Article 28. Masters of Soviet vessels that navigate abroad who have permitted the illegal stay on such vessels of persons who do not comprise their officers and crew or are not passengers shall bear responsibility for this.

III. Procedure for Protection of the State Boundary of the USSR

Article 29. Protection of the land and sea state boundary of the USSR shall be entrusted to the border guard, and the protection of the boundary of airspace of the USSR shall be entrusted to the anti-aircraft defense force (PVO).

In fulfilling the tasks of protection of the state boundary of the USSR, the border guard and PVO force shall be guided by prevailing legislation of the USSR and of the union republics, by agreements of the USSR with other states, by appropriate orders, instructions, and directions, and also by the Statute of the Armed Forces of the USSR.

Article 30. In protecting the state boundary of the USSR, the border guard, and in proper instances the anti-aircraft defense force, shall fulfill the following tasks:

a) repel armed intrusions on Soviet territory of military

groups and bands, and defend the border population and socialist and personal ownership from criminal infringements;

b) shall not permit crossings by foot or by conveyance on land or in the air of the state boundary in non-established places or by illegal means;

c) detain violators of the state boundary;

d) carry out at established points the admission of persons crossing the state boundary;

e) secure the protection of boundary markers and proper maintenance of the state boundary line of the USSR;

f) together with customs agencies, suppress the import or export across the boundary of objects, materials, currency, and negotiable valuables whose import and export is prohibited;

g) together with police agencies, control fulfillment of the rules of the boundary regime;

h) assist agencies of fishery supervision in the protection of sea and river wealth of the USSR from plunder by vessels which do not have permission for the right of trade, or which in conducting trade in territorial and internal sea waters of the USSR and the Soviet part of waters of border rivers and lakes have violated established rules;

i) watch over the observance by all vessels of the regime of navigation within the limits of territorial and internal sea waters of the USSR, as announced in Notices to Mariners.

Article 31. Within the limits of a boundary zone, a border belt, or administrative districts contiguous to the state boundary, the border guard shall have the right:

a) to position border details and to establish roadblocks, as well as in pursuing and detaining violators of the state boundary to move to any section of the locality. Pursuit of violators of the state boundary may also be made beyond the limits of the above-mentioned districts, zones, or belts on the territory of the USSR;

b) to escort trains and other means of transport with special border details;

c) to verify documents of persons found in a boundary zone or border belt, or, in pursuit and search of violators of the boundary beyond their limits;

d) to detain persons who have violated rules of the boundary regime and to transfer them to police agencies for prosecution;

e) to restrict temporarily the carrying out of various jobs directly on the boundary, excluding jobs of the Ministry of Defense of the USSR and on structures of general state significance, and also jobs connected with the liquidation of natural disasters (floods, earthquakes, fires, etc.);

f) to use existing telephone and telegraph lines of the Ministry of Communications of the USSR and of other ministries and departments in searching and detaining of violators of the boundary, under conditions agreed upon with local agencies of those ministries and departments.

Article 32. In cases concerning violations of the state boundary, the border guard shall enjoy the rights of investigative agencies, and in necessary instances shall take operational search measures and shall conduct urgent investigative actions: examination, search, seizure, examination of witnesses, detention and interrogation of violators of the boundary and their accomplices, and also interrogation of witnesses, being guided in this by criminal procedure law.

Article 33. The border guard shall be permitted, in the border belt, to erect special obstacles, to construct roads, bridges, gates, walls, and other installations necessary for border guard work, and to cut openings, by agreement with forestry agencies, and to clear bushes, rushes, and grass.

Article 34. In protecting the shores of seas and shores of border rivers and lakes, the right shall be accorded to the border guard, in the interests of protection of the boundary and taking into account the economic needs of collective farms, enterprises, and the local populace, to prohibit:

a) departure from shore on vessels and other means of navigation, and moorage thereto in non-established places or without proper permission;

b) employment and lighting on shore of fires which may be taken for beacons or distinctive lights of a vessel;

c) giving signals to vessels without a right to do so or in violation of established rules, excluding signals arising from an accident at sea;

d) moving along the shore or on ice outside the roads and paths established for this.

Article 35. Ships and other vessels of the border guard shall be permitted, if necessary, to sail at night without established lights within the limits of the territorial and internal sea waters of the USSR and of the Soviet part of waters of border rivers and lakes. In such instance commanders of the above-mentioned vessels shall be obliged to take necessary measures to prevent a collision with other vessels.

Article 36. With respect to foreign nonmilitary vessels, the border guard (or ships and other vessels) shall have the right, within the limits of the territorial and internal sea waters of the USSR, as well as of the Soviet part of waters of border rivers and lakes:

a) to propose to a vessel to show its national flag, if it is not raised, and to make an inquiry concerning the purposes of entry into these waters;

b) to propose to a vessel to change course, if it is in districts permanently or temporarily closed to navigation;

c) to stop a vessel and make an inspection, when it is situated in districts temporarily or permanently closed to navigation, is moving in territorial and internal sea waters of the USSR or in the Soviet part of waters of border rivers and lakes outside established channels or recommended courses, lies adrift, anchors, does not reply to signals of inquiry or change of course, as well as in all other instances when the vessel is situated in the above-mentioned waters in violation of rules established by the present Statute, or, being situated in such waters legally, permits a violation of the regime of stay in them.

Inspection of a vessel shall include verification of ship's and navigational documents, documents of the officers and crew, passengers, and cargo, and, in necessary instances, of the vessel's quarters.

In those instances when it has been established by inspection that the vessel is not subject to detention, it may be requested to leave USSR waters;

d) to place on a vessel, in necessary instances, a border detail to escort the vessel to port or from port to the line of the farthest extremity of territorial waters of the USSR;

e) to take from a vessel, and detain, persons who have committed criminal offenses and who are subject to criminal responsibility according to legislation of the USSR and of the union republics, and to transfer them to appropriate agencies. Such measures may not be applied to persons situated on board a foreign vessel passing through territorial waters of the USSR for crimes committed by them prior to entry of the vessel into territorial waters, if the vessel, in proceeding from a foreign port, restricts itself to passage through territorial waters and does not enter internal sea waters;

f) to pursue and detain a vessel which violates the state boundary of the USSR. In the event pursuit began in territorial or internal sea waters of the USSR and is conducted without interruption, the border guard shall have the right to continue it also on the high seas until such vessel enters its own or foreign territorial waters.

With respect to foreign warships, the provisions of the present article shall not apply but special rules shall prevail.

Article 37. Any foreign nonmilitary vessel situated in territorial and internal sea waters of the USSR, as well as in the Soviet part of the waters of border rivers and lakes, may be detained by ships and other vessels of the border guard and convoyed to the nearest port or pier, in instances:

a) when the vessel is situated in districts, announced in Notices to Mariners, permanently or temporarily closed to navigation;

b) when a vessel disembarks or embarks people or loads or unloads cargo in places not established therefor, if such actions are committed without the permission of competent agencies;

c) when a vessel illegally engages in maritime (or river) trade or hydrographic work and research in territorial and internal sea waters of the USSR as well as in the Soviet part of waters of border rivers and lakes;

d) when there is premeditated damaging of means of navigational barriers, communications cables, or other submerged or protruding objects belonging to the USSR, by members of the officers and crew of such vessels;

e) when the master of a vessel has not submitted the prescribed ship's and cargo documents;

f) when a vessel refuses to submit to orders of appropriate authorities of the USSR;

g) in all other instances when a vessel is situated in territorial and internal sea waters of the USSR or the Soviet part of waters of border rivers and lakes in violation of rules established by the present Statute or, being situated in these waters legally, permits violation of the regime of stay in them.

Article 38. An official document shall be drawn up concerning an inspection or detention of a vessel which shall be signed by the commander of the ship or other vessel of the border guard and by the master of the inspected or detained vessel. The official document shall be drawn up in the Russian language. If the master of the inspected or detained vessel requests that a copy of the official document be given to him, this must be given to him immediately. If circumstances prevent the immediate giving of a copy of the official document, it shall be sent to the address specified by the master of the inspected vessel.

In the event of detention of a vessel, all ship's and cargo documents shall be taken from the master, for whom a general inventory shall be drawn up. The documents shall be punched, laced with a string, and fastened together by the seals of the commander of the ship or other vessel of the border guard and master of the detained vessel, and shall be appended to the official document.

If the master of the inspected or detained vessel considers the actions of the commander of the ship or other vessel of the border guard to be incorrect or does not agree with the content of the official document, he may make a reservation on the same official document or in a separate document attached to the official document, in any language. Upon refusal of the master to sign the official document, an appropriate notation shall be made thereon.

Article 39. The border guard and PVO force, in carrying out protection of the state boundary of the USSR, shall use weapons to repel an armed attack on Soviet territory, and also shall have the right to use weapons against violators of the state boundary of the USSR on land, in water, and in the air, in instances when cessation of a violation or detention of violators may not be carried out by other means, or in response to the application of force on the part of violators.

Article 40. Local agencies of authority, and directors of state, cooperative, and other social organizations, shall be obliged to render all possible help to the border guard in the protection of the state boundary of the USSR.

With the cooperation of local soviet agencies and social organizations, the border guard may draw, on a voluntary basis, for assistance in protecting the boundary, upon Soviet citizens residing in populated border points, and in the first place upon the Volunteer People's Guard, on whose staffs shall be representatives of local agencies of the KGB, as well as of the border guard.

Appendix 11

RULES FOR VISITS BY FOREIGN WARSHIPS TO TERRITORIAL WATERS AND PORTS OF THE USSR

Adopted June 6, 1960. IM (1966), no. 14.

Article 1. A visit to territorial waters and ports of the USSR by foreign warships shall be permitted with the consent of the Government of the USSR.

Article 2. Consent for the entry of foreign warships shall be sought through the Ministry of Foreign Affairs of the USSR not later than 30 full days prior to the proposed visit, with notification of the following information: purpose of arrival, port of proposed visit, number, class, name, and basic measurements of ships (displacement, length, width, draught), duration of stay, military rank and surname of the commander (flag-officer).

Article 3. The directions of Articles 1 and 2 shall not extend to:

a) warships carrying heads of states or heads of governments and warships escorting them;

b) warships whose entry into Soviet territorial waters or ports of the USSR is performed as a consequence of natural disasters and damages which threaten the safety of the ship (forced entry). In such instances the foreign warship shall be obliged to notify the nearest port of the reason for entry into Soviet waters and, if possible, to go to one of the ports open for the entry of foreign merchant vessels or to a point specified by a ship of the VMF (Navy) or border guard sent to receive it or to render aid.

Article 4. As a general rule, the number of warships of the same state whose simultaneous stay shall be permitted in the same district of Soviet territorial waters or in the same port of the USSR must not exceed three. Unless the authorization it has received provides otherwise, the longest period of stay of each foreign warship in a Soviet port must not exceed seven full days.

Article 5. Visits by foreign warships to Soviet ports shall be divided into official visits, having as a basic purpose representational tasks and directed toward the development of friendly relations between states; unofficial visits, bringing, as a rule, training and scientific research ships and vessels; and arrivals arising from operational and technical circumstances.

The ceremony and order of reception of foreign warships in Soviet ports, the procedure for making salutes, and also the coordination of all questions connected with the paying of visits or making business calls to Soviet ports shall be determined by special instruction published by the Ministry of Defense of the USSR.

Article 6. Foreign warships shall be relieved of payment of port, ship's, and other charges in ports of the USSR, on condition of reciprocity. Charges shall be exacted only for services rendered (towing, pilot, etc.).

Warships shall also be relieved of customs inspection and customs duties. Customs duties shall be assessed only on goods unloaded on shore from the ship.

Article 7. Foreign submarines shall be permitted to enter and stay within the limits of the waters of the USSR only in a surface position.

Article 8. In visiting ports of the USSR, foreign warships shall be obliged to take pilots of the USSR in those ports on whose approaches pilot service is obligatory.

Article 9. While situated in territorial waters of the USSR, foreign warships must not enter districts closed to navigation. Such districts shall be announced in Notices to Mariners of the Hydrographic Service of the VMF (Navy).

Article 10. A communications officer, representing the senior maritime chief, shall board a foreign warship bound for a Soviet port at the approaches to the port.

At the direction of the commander of the foreign warship, the representative of the senior maritime chief who has boarded the ship shall transmit the information indicated in the list appended to the present rules (unless such information was transmitted previously). The representative of the senior maritime chief shall communicate those rules and instructions relating especially to foreign warships by which the warship, its cutter, sloops, and personnel must be guided during the stay in port (or in the roadstead).

Information concerning the sanitary condition of the warship shall be transmitted to the representative of sanitary supervision who has boarded the ship.

Note. In ports where there is no senior maritime chief or person specially appointed to replace him in receiving foreign warships, the rights and duties of a senior maritime chief shall be fulfilled by the chief of the garrison or senior chief of the local border guard agency.

Article 11. The place of anchorage of the foreign warship shall be designated by the senior maritime chief and shall be communicated by his representative to the commander of the ship upon their meeting.

If the representative of the senior maritime chief has not boarded the ship and the place for anchorage in the port is unknown to the commander of the foreign warship, the Commander of the ship shall inquire of port authorities about this, by radio or other means of communications, and shall anchor in accordance with their instructions. Later the senior maritime chief shall confirm, through his representative, the given anchorage of the ship or shall indicate to the commander of the foreign warship another place for anchorage and also all subsequent changes of anchorage if such changes are necessary.

Article 12. Unarmed cutters and sloops of foreign warships may move about within the limits of the port only in accordance with the rules and instructions of the senior maritime chief established in the port.

Article 13. Shore leave for personnel of foreign warships shall be made according to an agreement with the senior maritime chief indicating the number of those on leave and time of departure and return to the ship in accordance with rules established in the port.

Article 14. Upon arrival on shore, the personnel of foreign warships must observe the rules for wearing uniforms.

Personnel may not go on shore with a weapon, except for officers, for whom the wearing of sidearms is permitted if it is a custom of their dress.

Article 15. Persons not comprising the officers and crew of a foreign warship shall be admitted aboard the ship and to go back ashore as provided by the senior maritime chief in agreement with the commander of the ship and with observance of the proper passport and customs rules of the USSR.

Note. Special instructions of the Ministry of Defense of the USSR, agreed upon with the Ministry of Foreign Affairs of the USSR, shall prevail with respect to diplomatic and consular representatives of the country to which the arriving foreign warship belongs.

Article 16. In the course of a visit to territorial waters and ports of the USSR, foreign warships and their personnel may not perform, in addition to actions prohibited by other laws and rules, the following:

a) research and investigations, as well as soundings and fathomings other than those necessary for the safe navigation of the ship in channels open for navigation to all ships, or for its safe anchorage at the place designated in the port;

b) photographic and other forms of sketches, drawings, copies, and compilation of descriptions of any districts of ports, as well as of fortifications and all military and other installations;

c) displacement of armed cutters, sloops, and sloop exercises with an armed crew or landing party;

d) exercises with a searchlight;

e) firing of any types of weapons (except salutes);

f) laying or sweeping of mines;

g) exercises involving the use of chemical substances, laying of smoke screens, creation of artificial clouds;

h) any kind of underwater explosions;

i) performance of flights, use of aerostats, kites, etc.;

j) use of radio-sounding and other radiotechnical and acoustical means, etc., upon anchoring in port;

k) catching of any kind of fish or marine life;

1) pollution of water by discharges of oil and other substances.

Article 17. In accordance with a preliminary request, the commander of a foreign warship may be permitted by the senior maritime chief:

a) to use wireless radio transmission equipment for communications with his own country;

b) to do underwater work connected with the inspection or repair of the foreign warship;

c) to bring the command together in formation, on shore, with weapons or without, for making rounds or for participation in parades or funeral ceremonies.

Article 18. In the event of violation of the established rules by the warship or its personnel, the attention of the commander of the foreign warship shall be called thereto by the senior maritime chief or the official replacing him, and at the same time the command shall be informed of the nature of the violation. A foreign warship which disregards a warning may be requested to leave the territorial waters of the USSR by order of the proper authorities.

In exceptional circumstances, a foreign warship may be requested at any time to leave the territorial waters of the USSR for a determined interval.

Article 19. The present rules shall extend to auxiliary naval vessels as well as to armed vessels for the protection of fisheries.

Article 20. The "Provisional Rules for Foreign Warships Visiting Waters of the USSR" of February 25, 1931, shall be considered to have lost their force.

Annex to Article 10.

List of Information to be Received from Foreign Warships

1. Nationality (or flag) and class (or type).
2. Name of ship (or ships).
3. Rank and surname of commander (or flag-officer).
4. Number (or list) of officers.
5. Numbers of petty officers and rank and file.
6. Purpose (or reason) of visit (only for ships whose entry is performed as a consequence of natural disaster or damage).
7. Last port from which the ship came.
8. Time of stay:
   a) arrival;
   b) departure.
9. Main data of the ship:
   a) displacement (or for submarines, surface and submerged, or vessels which have arrived in port for performance of commercial operations, data concerning gross and net tonnage of the vessel);
   b) length;
   c) draught.
10. Armament:
   a) artillery;
   b) rocket and jet;
   c) torpedo;
   d) mines (only for ships whose entry is performed as a consequence of natural disaster or damage).
11. Presence of airplanes or helicopters (number, type).
12. Sanitary condition:
   a) ship and personnel;
   b) port of departure.
13. List of passengers (if any).
14. Nature and quantity of cargo (delivered or unloaded), if there is cargo.

. . .

Note. The list of information shall be drawn up in the Russian language or the language of the country to which the warship belongs.

Appendix 12

FUNDAMENTAL PRINCIPLES OF SOVIET CIVIL LEGISLATION

December 8, 1961. Vedomosti SSSR (1961), no. 50, item 525.

(Excerpt)

Part I. General Provisions

Article 1. Tasks of Soviet Civil Legislation.

Soviet civil legislation shall regulate property relations and related non-property personal relations for the purpose of creating the material and technical basis for communism and providing ever fuller satisfaction of the material and spiritual requirements of citizens. In instances provided for by law, civil legislation shall also regulate other non-property relations.

Property relations in Soviet society shall be based on the socialist system of economy and socialist ownership of the means and instruments of production. The economic development of the USSR shall be determined and guided by the state national economic plan.

Article 2. Relations Regulated by the Fundamental Principles of Soviet Civil Legislation.

The Fundamental Principles of Soviet Civil Legislation shall regulate the relations specified in Article 1 of the present Fundamental Principles:

between state, cooperative, and social organizations;
between citizens and state, cooperative, and social organizations;
between citizens.

Other organizations may also be parties to relations regulated by Soviet civil legislation in instances provided for by legislation of the USSR.

The civil legislation of the USSR and union republics shall not apply to property relations based on the administrative subordination of one party to another, or to tax and budget relations.

Family, labor, and land relations, as well as relations within collective farms arising from their charters, shall be regulated respectively by family, labor, land, and collective farm legislation.

Article 3. Civil Legislation of the USSR and Union Republics.

In accordance with the present Fundamental Principles, the civil codes and other acts of civil legislation of union republics shall regulate property and non-property personal relations, both provided for and not provided for by the Fundamental Principles.

In conformity with the present Fundamental Principles, the civil legislation of the USSR shall regulate relations between socialist organizations in delivery of products, and capital construction; relations involving state purchases of agricultural produce from collective and state farms; relations between organizations in railway, sea, river, air, and pipeline transport, and communications and credit establishments, and their clients, and between themselves; relations in state insurance; relations arising from discoveries, inventions, and technical improvements; as well as other relations whose regulation is referred by the Constitution of the USSR and the present Fundamental Principles to the jurisdiction of the USSR. Within the sphere of these relations, the legislation of union republics may decide matters referred to their jurisdiction by the legislation of the USSR.

Foreign trade relations shall be determined by special legislation of the USSR regulating foreign trade, and by the general civil legislation of the USSR and union republics.

. . .

Appendix 13

CUSTOMS CODE OF THE USSR

May 5, 1964. Vedomosti SSSR (1964), no. 20, item 242.

(Excerpt)

. . .

Article 35. Warships shall not be subject to customs examination.

By warship, in the present Code, is meant any vessel (or auxiliary vessel) sailing under a military or border guard flag, under the command of a person in military service or on the staff of a military command, as well as a vessel which in accordance with a special declaration of the Ministry of Defense of the USSR performs tasks of a military-operational nature.

The commander of a warship shall bear responsibility for observance of the provisions of the present Code.

Article 36. The rules of Article 35 of the present Code shall extend also to foreign warships during a visit to ports of the USSR.

. . .

Appendix 14

PROCLAMATION REGARDING FORTIFIED ZONES AND RULES OF NAVIGATION THEREIN

IM, (1966), no. 4.

Sometimes it may be necessary to establish a special regime of navigation for waters which is not provisional, but permanent, in certain areas contiguous to the Union of Soviet Socialist Republics. These areas shall be termed "fortified zones" below.

All vessels sailing in waters contiguous to the Union of Soviet Socialist Republics shall be obliged to adhere strictly to the "Rules of Navigation in Fortified Zones of the USSR" announced below.

Data pertaining to areas announced as fortified zones shall be published in the Notices to Mariners of the Naval Hydrographic Service.

Rules of Navigation in Fortified Zones of the USSR.

1. The present rules shall extend to all USSR and foreign merchant vessels that navigate abroad.

2. Fortified zones shall be announced in Notices to Mariners of the Naval Hydrographic Service, and reference to lack of knowledge thereof may not serve as a ground for avoidance of responsibility for their violation.

3. No USSR or foreign merchant ship that navigates abroad may enter or depart from a fortified zone without previous authorization to do so.

When it is necessary to traverse a fortified zone in order to enter one of the ports open to merchant vessels that navigate abroad, the procedure of entry into a fortified zone shall be governed in each individual instance by a special notification.

4. In any event, the passage of a merchant vessel through fortified zones without a pilot is prohibited.

While traversing a fortified zone, the master of a vessel is obliged to fulfill immediately all instructions of the pilot pertaining to questions connected with safeguarding the regime of navigation in the given zone. (black-out, removal of personnel from the main deck, etc.)

5. At night all merchant vessels should pass through a fortified zone only with prescribed lights, unless special notification has been given for the black-out of vessels or the pilot has given instructions concerning this.

In the daytime vessels shall be obliged to bear an ensign, a pennant of the steamship-line (or company), and their ship's number.

6. All vessels passing through a fortified zone shall be prohibited from anchoring closer than three cable lengths from the axis of a marked channel and recommended course.

7. Merchant vessels in all instances shall be obliged to yield the right of way to formations of warships, not to cut through their formation, and not to approach warships conducting special exercises or firing.

Clear passage of individual warships not engaged in conducting special exercises must be carried out in accordance with the PPSS. (Rules for Prevention of Collision of Ships at Sea - ed.)

8. With the approach of fog, the passage of merchant vessels through fortified zones shall be prohibited.

Appendix 15

LIST OF PORTS AND ROADSTEADS OPEN TO FOREIGN VESSELS

IM, (1966), no. 12.

I. Arctic Ocean

1. Murmansk
2. Umba
3. Kovda
4. Keret
5. Kem
6. Onega
7. Archangel
8. Mezen
9. Narian-Mar
10. Igarka

II. Baltic Sea

1. Leningrad
2. Vysotsk
3. Vyborg
4. Piarnu
5. Riga
6. Ventspils
7. Klaipeda

III. Black Sea

1. Reni
2. Izmail
3. Kiliia
4. Belgorod-Dnestrovskii
5. Ilichevsk
6. Odessa
7. Kherson
8. Novorossiisk
9. Tuapse
10. Poti
11. Batumi

IV. Sea of Azov

1. Zhdanov
2. Berdiansk

V. Pacific Ocean

1. Nakhodka
2. Aleksandrovsk-Sakhalinskii
3. Makarevskii Roadstead
4. Oktiabrskii
5. Shakhtersk
6. Uglegorsk
7. Kholmsk
8. Nevelsk
9. Makarova Roadstead
10. Poronaisk Roadstead

Appendix 16

PROCLAMATION REGARDING PROHIBITED AREAS OF NAVIGATION AND ANCHORING

IM, (1966), no. 4.

Sometimes it is necessary to prohibit the navigation and anchoring of vessels in waters of certain coastal areas of the USSR. In those instances the boundaries of areas in which navigation and anchoring of all vessels without exception is prohibited shall be announced in Notices to Mariners of the Naval Hydrographic Service.

These areas shall be announced as prohibited for a definite period of time, temporarily as a rule, and shall be termed "areas temporarily prohibited for navigation."

Areas in which only anchoring is prohibited are permanent and shall be termed "areas prohibited for anchoring."

The boundaries of these prohibited areas are subject to being plotted on maps according to Notices to Mariners of the Naval Hydrographic Service.

Appendix 17

PROCEDURE FOR NAVIGATION OF VESSELS IN THE VILKITSKII AND SHOKALSKII STRAITS

IM, (1966), no. 5.

Compulsory icebreaker conducting and pilotage of all vessels shall be introduced in the Vilkitskii and Shokalskii Straits for the purpose of ensuring safety of navigation in view of the highly complicated navigational and ice conditions.

Appendix 18

PUBLICATION OF DATA RECEIVED FROM FOREIGN SOURCES

IM, (1966), no. 8.

The Hydrographic Service of the Navy of the USSR shall publish rules, directions, and announcements of foreign states pertaining to questions of navigation, as well as information concerning battle training areas and weapons testing areas, which have been published in foreign notices to mariners and other publications, in its Notices to Mariners, and in navigation manuals.

The Hydrographic Service of the Navy shall make clear that this data is published only for the purpose of information for masters of Soviet vessels in order to ensure safety of navigation.

The fact of publication of the aforementioned data in Notices to Mariners in no way signifies that these rules, directions, and announcements of foreign states, as well as the battle training areas and weapons testing areas established by them, are legal from the standpoint of international law or to any degree recognized by the Government of the Soviet Union.

In publishing this data, the Hydrographic Service of the Navy may not bear responsibility for possible incompleteness of information and possible inaccuracies of any rules, directions, and announcements or certain details contained in the said foreign sources.

B INTERNATIONAL TREATIES AND AGREEMENTS

Appendix 19

GENEVA CONVENTION ON THE TERRITORIAL SEA AND CONTIGUOUS ZONE

April 29, 1958. Vedomosti SSSR (1964), no. 43, item 472.

Reservations of the USSR

To Article 20: The Government of the USSR considers that state vessels in foreign territorial waters enjoy immunity, and therefore the application of measures mentioned in the present article to them may occur only with the consent of the state under whose flag the ships sail.

To Article 23: (Subsection D. The Rule as applied to warships) The Government of the USSR considers that a coastal state has the right to establish an authorization procedure for the passage of foreign warships through its territorial waters.

Appendix 20

AGREEMENT BETWEEN THE GOVERNMENT OF THE UNION OF SOVIET SOCIALIST REPUBLICS AND THE GOVERNMENT OF THE REPUBLIC OF FINLAND REGARDING FISHING AND SEALING

Signed at Moscow, February 21, 1959. 338 UNTS 3.

(Excerpt)

The Government of the Union of Soviet Socialist Republics and the Government of the Republic of Finland,

Having regard to the favorable development of relations between the USSR and Finland, founded on the 1948 Treaty of Friendship, Cooperation and Mutual Assistance between the Union of Soviet Socialist Republics and the Republic of Finland,

Considering that the Government of the Soviet Union, in compliance with the wishes of the Government of the Republic of Finland, has expressed its willingness to permit Finnish fishermen to engage in fishing and sealing in the territorial waters of the Soviet Union in the Gulf of Finland,

Have decided to conclude this Agreement and have appointed their plenipotentiaries, who, having exchanged their full powers, found in good and due form, have agreed as follows:

Article 1. The Government of the Union of Soviet Socialist Republics agrees to permit Finnish nationals resident in the communes of Virolahti, Vehkalahti and Haapasaari to engage in fishing and sealing in the territorial waters of the Soviet Union in the Gulf of Finland within an area bounded by a line passing through the following points:

(1) Latitude 60° 15' 15", longitude 27° 30' 29" --terminal point in the Gulf of Finland of the State boundary between the Soviet Union and Finland, which is indicated by boundary mark No. 14;
(2) Latitude 60° 15' 15", longitude 27° 43' 48";
(3) Latitude 60° 23' 28", longitude 27° 50' 18";
(4) Latitude 60° 23' 29", longitude 27° 43' 45"--turning point of the State boundary between the Soviet Union and Finland, which is indicated by boundary mark No. 10,

as shown in the chart annexed to this Agreement (Annex 1).*

Finnish vessels, in proceeding to the said area for purposes of fishing or sealing and in returning therefrom, shall cross the State boundary of the Soviet Union in the section of that boundary extending from boundary mark No. 10 to the point marked by a buoy situated at latitude 60° 22' 0" and longitude 27° 41' 10".

For the guidance of fishermen, that portion of the Soviet territorial waters in which Finnish fishermen are permitted under this Agreement to engage in fishing and sealing shall be marked off by the Soviet Party with buoys and spar buoys, the coordinates of which shall be indicated in the notices issued for navigators.

---

* The Annexes are not reproduced.

Article 2. Finnish fishermen may engage in fishing and sealing in that portion of Soviet territorial waters covered by this Agreement from July 1 to November 1 during the summer fishing-season, and from January 1 to April 20 during the winter fishing-season.

During the summer fishing-season, the permitted types of fishing shall be net fishing from motor boats and rowboats, fishing by means of small trawls and fishing by hook and line.

During the winter fishing-season, net fishing may be carried on underneath the ice, and fishermen's huts may be brought to the fishing site and used there for dwelling purposes.

Article 3. Finnish vessels engaged in fishing and sealing in the area covered by this Agreement shall, having regard to the provisions of this Agreement, be subject to the rules governing fishing and sealing in Soviet waters and to the laws and regulations of the Soviet Union relating to the presence of foreign vessels and foreign nationals in Soviet territorial waters.

Particulars of such laws, regulations and rules and of amendments and additions thereto shall be notified to the Finnish Party through the diplomatic channel.

Article 4. Finnish nationals engaged in fishing and sealing in the area covered by this Agreement shall have with them the following documents, which shall be drawn up in the Russian and Finnish languages:

(a) A fishing pass made out in the name of the owner of the vessel or horse-drawn vehicle (Annex 2) and constituting permission to engage in fishing or sealing in the area covered by this Agreement;

(b) A freedom of movement permit (Annex 3), which must be in the possession of every person on board the vessel or in the horse-drawn vehicle.

Every person transporting a catch of fish or seals from the fisheries area shall likewise be required to have a freedom of movement permit;

(c) A list of fishing gear and other articles carried.

The documents specified in sub-paragraphs (a) and (b) of this Article shall be issued by the competent Finnish authorities and shall, together with the list referred to in paragraph (c), be certified by the Finnish border-control authorities.

The fishing pass, freedom of movement permit, and list of fishing gear and cargo shall be produced to the Soviet authorities upon request.

Article 5. The letter "S" and the fishing-pass number shall be painted in white characters on a black ground, the said characters being at least fifteen centimeters high and at least nine centimeters wide, on both sides of the bow of every vessel engaged in fishing or sealing in the area covered by this Agreement. The home port of the vessel shall be shown on the stern.

Article 6. A list, certified by the Finnish border authorities, of the persons to whom the documents referred to in Article 4 have been issued and a list of the fishing vessels and their numerical markings shall be transmitted by the said Finnish border authorities to the Soviet border authorities, through the border commissioners, not later than fifteen days before the beginning of each fishing season.

Article 7. Where necessary in order to ensure the safety of winter fishing and sealing operations and to prevent damage to fishing gear from movements of the ice, the competent Finnish fisheries organization may dispatch to the area covered by this Agreement its rescue vessel stationed at Huovari Island, the said vessel being subject in all respects to the provisions of this Agreement.

Article 8. In the area covered by this Agreement, fishing gear shall be considered to be adequately marked if, when drift-nets are being used, one end of the set of nets is attached to the vessel and the other end is marked with two signals. When fishing is carried on with fixed nets, two signals shall be attached to each end of the set of nets. In the case both of drift-net fishing and of fishing with fixed nets, the inner signals of the set of nets shall consist of white flags, and the outer signals, of red flags. The said flags shall measure 30 X 60 centimeters and shall be attached to floats rising at least two meters above the surface of the water.

Additional signals without flags shall be placed at intervals of 100 meters in the center of each set of nets.

During the hours of darkness, the nets shall be marked with white signal-lights visible in all directions. The signal-lights shall be placed not less than 70 centimeters above the surface of the water and shall be visible for a distance of one nautical mile.

Article 9. Compensation claims in respect of physical damage caused, in the area covered by this Agreement, to the Soviet Party by Finnish nationals in consequence of a contravention of the fishing and sealing rules shall be submitted by the Leningrad Economic Council to the Agricultural Administration of Finland.

Compensation claims in respect of physical damage caused, in the area covered by this Agreement, to the Finnish Party by Soviet nationals in consequence of a contravention of the fishing and sealing rules shall be submitted by the Agricultural Administration of Finland to the Leningrad Economic Council.

Article 10. Finnish nationals who, in fishing or sealing in the area covered by this Agreement, contravene the provisions of this Agreement may be deprived by the competent Soviet authorities of the right of engaging in fishing or sealing in the said area.

Article 11. This Agreement shall be ratified. The instruments of ratification shall be exchanged as soon as possible at Helsinki.

The Agreement has been concluded for a period of five years and shall come into force on the date on which the instruments of ratification are exchanged.

If, within not less than six months before the end of the said five-year period of validity, neither Contracting Party gives notice of its desire to terminate the Agreement, the Agreement shall remain in force for an additional year and so on each year throughout an additional period of five years, on condition that either Contracting Party may terminate the Agreement by giving notice to that effect within not less than six months before the end of the current one-year period of validity.

If, however, the termination becomes effective during a fishing season, the provisions of the Agreement shall remain in force until the end of such season.

Done in Moscow on February 21, 1959, in duplicate in the Russian and Finnish languages, both texts being equally authentic.

For the Government of the Union of Soviet Socialist Republics:

V. Zorin

For the Government of the Republic of Finland:

Eero A. Wuori

Appendix 21

PROTOCOL REGARDING EXTENSION OF THE FINNISH-SOVIET AGREEMENT OF FEBRUARY 21, 1959, REGARDING FISHING AND SEALING IN THE AREA OF THE GULF OF FINLAND TO THE EAST OF SURSARI (GOGLAND) ISLAND

Signed at Helsinki, May 20, 1965.

The Government of the Republic of Finland and the Government of the Union of Soviet Socialist Republics,

Having regard to the favorable development of relations between Finland and the USSR, founded on the 1948 Finnish-Soviet Treaty of Friendship, Cooperation, and Mutual Assistance and the Agreement Regarding the Boundaries of Sea Waters and the Continental Shelf in the Gulf of Finland between the Contracting Parties signed today,

Having in view that the Government of the Union of Soviet Socialist Republics, in meeting the desires of the Government of the Republic of Finland, expressed a readiness to accord to Finnish nationals the right to engage in fishing and sealing in the area of Soviet territorial waters in the Gulf of Finland to the east of Sursari (Gogland) Island,

Considering the Agreement between the Government of the Republic of Finland and the Government of the Union of Soviet Socialist Republics Regarding Fishing and Sealing of February 21, 1959,

Have decided to conclude the present Protocol and have appointed their plenipotentiaries who, having exchanged their credentials, found to be in official form and proper order, have agreed upon the following.

Article 1. The Government of the Union of Soviet Socialist Republics agrees to accord to nationals of the Republic of Finland the right to engage in fishing and sealing in the area of Soviet territorial waters in the Gulf of Finland to the east of Sursari (Gogland) Island on the terms provided for in the Finnish-Soviet Agreement Regarding Fishing and Sealing of February 21, 1959, and in letters which the Parties exchanged on February 21, 1959, upon signing the Agreement indicated.

A new area in which the right to engage in fishing and sealing is accorded to Finnish nationals shall be bounded by the lines passing through the following points:

1. Latitude 60° 13' 42", longitude 27° 27' 50";
2. Latitude 60° 12' 19", longitude 27° 18' 01";
3. Latitude 60° 08' 49", longitude 27° 04' 36";
4. Latitude 60° 08' 49", longitude 27° 27' 50",

as shown on maritime chart No. 403, 1964 edition, appended to the present Protocol.

The aforementioned Finnish-Soviet Agreement of February 21, 1959, hereinafter "Agreement," shall apply to fishing and sealing in the new area with the changes set forth in Articles 2-8 of the present Protocol.

Article 2. The right to engage in fishing and sealing in the new area shall be accorded to all nationals of the Republic of Finland on condition of their observing the provisions of the Agreement and the present Protocol.

Article 3. Fishing shall be permitted throughout the entire year with the use of trawls, nets, and fishing by hook and line. Sealing also shall be permitted during this same period.

Article 4. Lists of persons and vessels engaged in fishing or sealing during the half-year beginning January 1 and July 1 must be transmitted by Finnish frontier authorities to Soviet frontier authorities not later than 15 days prior to the beginning of the half year indicated.

Article 5. The frontier authorities of the Republic of Finland shall notify the frontier authorities of the Union of Soviet Socialist Republics regarding all Finnish vessels sailing to engage in fishing or sealing in the area specified in Article 1 of the present Protocol.

Article 6. Finnish vessels sailing to engage in fishing and sealing in the aforementioned area may cross the state boundary of the USSR in the section from the points latitude 60°13'42", longitude 27°27'50", and latitude 60°08'49", longitude 27°04' 36".

Article 7. Necessary clarifications shall be made in the passes, documents, and lists provided for in the Agreement which show that they apply to fishing or sealing in the area defined in the present Protocol.

Article 8. The present Protocol is subject to ratification. The exchange of ratification instruments shall take place as soon as possible in Moscow.

The protocol has been concluded for a period of five years and shall enter into force on the day the ratification instruments are exchanged.

If neither Contracting Party gives notice of denunciation of the present Protocol not later than six months before the end of the said five year period, it shall remain in force for an additional year and so on each year throughout an additional period of five years. Each Party may denounce the Protocol, having given notice not later than six months before the end of the current one year period of validity of the Protocol.

Done at Helsinki, May 20, 1965, in duplicate, each in the Finnish and Russian languages, both texts being equally authentic.

Appendix 22

AGREEMENT BETWEEN THE GOVERNMENT OF THE REPUBLIC OF FINLAND AND THE GOVERNMENT OF THE UNION OF SOVIET SOCIALIST REPUBLICS REGARDING THE BOUNDARIES OF SEA WATERS AND THE CONTINENTAL SHELF IN THE GULF OF FINLAND

Signed at Helsinki, May 20, 1965.

The Government of the Republic of Finland and the Government of the Union of Soviet Socialist Republics,

Having regard to the favorable development of relations between Finland and the Soviet Union, founded on the 1948 Finnish-Soviet Treaty of Friendship, Cooperation, and Mutual Assistance, and the interests of Finnish fishermen,

Desiring to delimit the sea waters and continental shelf in the Gulf of Finland as well as to promote the further development of good-neighborly relations between both countries,

Considering the 1958 Geneva Conventions on the Territorial Sea and Contiguous Zone and on the Continental Shelf,

Have decided to conclude the present Agreement and have appointed their plenipotentiaries, who have signed below, and who, having exchanged their credentials, found to be in official form and proper order, have agreed upon the following.

Article 1. The Contracting Parties agree to the following sea boundary line between Finland and the USSR, as well as the boundary lines of Finnish and Soviet territorial waters in the Gulf of Finland in the section to the northeast of Sursari (Gogland) Island:

The sea boundary line between the Republic of Finland and the Union of Soviet Socialist Republics established in 1940 and affirmed by the 1947 Peace Treaty with Finland from the terminal point of the sea boundary at latitude 60°15'35", longitude 27°30'43" passes along a straight line in a southwest direction to the point at latitude 60°13'42", longitude 27°27'50", and then turns and passes along a straight line in a west-southwest direction to the point at latitude 60°12'19", longitude 27°18'01", which shall be the terminal point of the sea boundary between Finland and the Soviet Union.

The boundary line of Soviet territorial waters passes from the aforementioned point of the sea boundary along a straight line in a southwest direction to a point at latitude 60°08'49", longitude 27°04'36", located on the boundary lines of Soviet territorial waters established in 1940 and affirmed by the 1947 Peace Treaty with Finland.

The boundary line of Finnish territorial waters passes from the aforementioned terminal point of the sea boundary along a straight line in a westerly direction to a point at latitude 60°12'19", longitude 27°13'49", located on the boundary line of Finnish territorial waters established in 1940 and affirmed by the 1947 Peace Treaty with Finland.

Article 2. The Contracting Parties agree not to broaden their fishing and other zones in the Gulf of Finland to the north of Sursari (Gogland) Island beyond the line intersecting the water expanses between the boundaries of Finnish and Soviet territorial waters established in 1940 and affirmed by the 1947 Peace Treaty with Finland.

The line specified shall begin from the point at latitude 60°10,6', longitude 27°11,3' and pass in a general westerly direction through the points at latitude 60°10,6', longitude 26°57,9', latitude 60°10,4', longitude 26°54,9' to the point at 60°08,8', longitude 26°47,9', which shall be the beginning point of a median line in the Gulf of Finland to the west of Sursari (Gogland) Island.

Article 3. The Contracting Parties agree not to broaden their territorial waters, as well as fishing and other zones, in the Gulf of Finland to the west of Sursari (Gogland) Island beyond the median line passing through the points with the following geographic coordinates:

Lat. 60°08,8', long. 26°47,9'; lat. 60°06,8', long. 26°38,4'; lat. 60°06,4', long. 26°32,6'; lat. 60°00,0', long. 26°20,8'; lat. 59°59,4', long. 26°13,1'; lat. 59°58,4', long. 26°08,4'; lat. 59°52,0', long. 25°58,5'; lat. 59°52,9', long. 25°28,0'; lat. 59°53,6', long. 25°10,6'; lat. 59°52,4', long. 24°57,6'; lat. 59°50,8', long. 24°49,7'; lat. 59°44,5', long. 24°24,8'; lat. 59°37,4', long. 23°54,8'; lat. 59°31,9', long. 23°30,1'; lat. 59°32,0', long. 23°10,0'.

Article 4. The sea boundary lines, the boundaries of Finnish and Soviet territorial waters specified in Article 1, as well as the lines mentioned in Articles 2 and 3 with indications of geographic coordinates through which these lines pass, have been plotted on maritime charts, numbers 400, 403, and 404, 1964 edition, and appended to the present Agreement. All coordinates in the present Agreement have been given in the coordinate system of these maritime charts.

Article 5. The Contracting Parties shall mark places of turning and terminal points of the sea boundary between the Republic of Finland and the Union of Soviet Socialist Republics corresponding to geographic coordinates, latitude 60°13'42", longitude 27°27'50", as well as latitude 60°12, 19", longitude 27°18'01".

Expenses connected with carrying out the specified work shall be apportioned equally between the Contracting Parties.

Article 6. The lines specified in Articles 2 and 3 of the present Agreement shall be the boundaries of the continental shelf of the Republic of Finland and the Union of Soviet Socialist Republics in the Gulf of Finland.

Article 7. The present Agreement is subject to ratification and shall enter into force on the day following the exchange of ratification instruments.

The exchange of ratification instruments shall take place in Moscow within the shortest possible period.

Done at Helsinki, May 20, 1965, in duplicate, each in the Finnish and Russian languages, both texts being equally authentic.

For the Government of the Republic of Finland

Pentti Suomela

For the Government of the Union of Soviet Socialist Republics

O. Khlestov

Appendix 23

TREATY OF FRIENDSHIP BETWEEN THE RUSSIAN SOCIALIST FEDERATED SOVIET REPUBLIC AND PERSIA (IRAN)

February 26, 1921. 2 SDD 36-41.

(Excerpt)

. . .

Article 1. The Soviet Government of Russia, in accordance with its declarations regarding Russian policy towards the people of Persia, set forth in notes of January 14, 1918, and June 26, 1919, declares again that it renounces absolutely the policy of oppression followed with respect to Persia by the imperialist governments of Russia, which were overthrown by the will of its laborers and peasants.

In accordance with the above and the desire to see the people of Persia become independent and prosperous and to freely use their property, the Soviet Government of Russia proclaims that all treaties, agreements, and conventions concluded by the former Tsarist Government with Persia, by which the former impaired the rights of the people of Persia, are abrogated and have lost force.

. . .

Article 5. Both High Contracting Parties undertake:

1. Not to permit the formation or residence on their territories of organizations or groups, of whatever name, or of individual persons, there for the purpose of struggle against Persia and Russia, as well as against states allied with the latter, and also not to permit the enlistment of men for the army or the mobilization of soldiers for any detachments or for the armed forces of these organizations.

2. To prohibit any state or organization, whatever its name, there for the purpose of struggle against the other High Contracting Party, from importing into or transporting through its territory, anything which may be used against the other High Contracting Party.

3. Not to permit the access to its territory of an army or armed forces of any third state, if the sojourn of these forces may threaten the border, interests, or security of the other High Contracting Party.

Article 6. Both High Contracting Parties have agreed that in the event a third country intends to pursue a policy of armed intervention on Persian territory or to transform Persian territory into a base for military attacks against Russia, or thereby to threaten the security of the boundaries of the Russian Socialist Federated Soviet Republic or powers allied with it, and if the Persian Government, after having been warned by the Soviet Government of Russia, is not able to remove this danger itself, the Soviet Government of Russia shall have the right to send its army onto the territory of Persia in order, in the interests of self-defense, to take necessary military measures. Upon the elimination of the danger, the Soviet Government of Russia is obliged to immediately withdraw its army from Persia.

Article 7. In view of the fact that the provisions set forth in Article 6 are equally applicable with respect to security in the Caspian Sea, both High Contracting Parties have agreed that should there be nationals of third powers among the officers and crew of vessels of the Persian navy who would use their presence in the Persian navy for purposes unfriendly with respect to Russia, the Soviet Government of Russia shall have the right to demand of the Persian Government the removal of the said hostile elements.

. . .

Article 11. In view of the fact that the principles involved in Article 1 of this Treaty abrogate the Treaty concluded between Persia and Russia at Turkmanchai on February 19, 1908, which Treaty deprived Persia of the right to have a fleet on the Caspian Sea, the High Contracting Parties have agreed that from the date of the signing of this Treaty the two powers shall have equal rights in navigation on the Caspian Sea under their respective flags.

. . .

Appendix 24

TREATY REGARDING TRADE AND NAVIGATION BETWEEN THE UNION OF SOVIET SOCIALIST REPUBLICS AND IRAN

March 25, 1940. 10 SDD 56.

(Excerpt)

. . .

Article 12. 1. Merchant vessels sailing under the flag of one of the Contracting Parties in the Caspian Sea shall be treated in ports of the other Party upon their entry, during their stay, and upon departure, in the same way in all respects as national vessels.

2. The said vessels shall not pay any port charges except those legally established for national vessels, on the same terms and with the same exceptions.

In exacting the aforementioned charges, the following shall not be considered to be imported or exported goods:

a) Passengers' baggage which is not part of the cargo; in addition to small hand luggage, passengers' baggage also includes articles transported on luggage receipts;

b) Fuel, provisions for passengers and crew, and ships' supplies and stores in quantity necessary for the voyage, provided these are not unloaded from the vessel and left in port;

c) Cargo unloaded because of damage to the vessel or left in port during other emergencies, if it is afterwards reloaded for purposes of transport to its port of destination;

d) Cargo carried by vessels of less than 3 1/2 tons register;

e) Cargo reloaded onto other vessels for further transport by sea.

3. Coastal trade shall be reserved for national vessels of the Contracting Parties. It is understood, however, that each of the Contracting Parties shall accord to vessels under the flag of the other Party the right of coastal trade for transporting passengers and cargoes in the Caspian Sea.

4. Irrespective of the preceding provision, each of the Contracting Parties shall retain for vessels of its own flag the fishing rights in waters washing its shores up to a limit of ten miles, as well as the right to enjoy the exemptions and privileges with respect to the import of fish caught by the crews of vessels sailing under its flag.

5. In seas other than the Caspian, vessels sailing under the flag of one of the Contracting Parties shall enjoy in the territorial waters and ports of the other Party with respect to conditions of navigation, including charges of any type, the same rights and privileges as are accorded to vessels of the most-favored state.

6. Tugs which have other vessels in tow shall be exempt from payment of port (or tonnage) charges.

Article 13. The Contracting Parties are agreed that in accordance with the principles set forth by the treaty of February 26, 1921, between the Russian Socialist Federated Soviet Republic and Persia, only vessels belonging to the Union of Soviet Socialist Republics or Iran, and likewise to nationals and commercial and transport organizations of either of the Contracting Parties, sailing under the flag of the Union of Soviet Socialist Republics or Iran respectively, may be found throughout the Caspian Sea.

Article 14. Tonnage certificates issued to vessels sailing in the Caspian Sea respectively under the flag of the Union of Soviet Socialist Republics or Iran by competent agencies of the Contracting Parties, about which each Party shall notify the other, shall be reciprocally recognized in the ports of both Parties. Vessels having such tonnage certificates shall not be subject to a new inspection in the ports of the other Party. Likewise, certificates of seaworthiness and of load line issued to the vessels by the aforementioned agencies, and all other navigation documents of a technical character, shall be reciprocally recognized in the ports of both Contracting Parties situated on the Caspian Sea.

Article 15. The Contracting Parties agree that with respect to sanitary measures to be applied to vessels of either in the ports of the other Party in the Caspian Sea, the provisions of the International Sanitary Convention signed in Paris on June 26, 1926, shall be applicable, with due regard to the reservations made by each of the Contracting Parties upon signing that Convention.

. . .

Appendix 25

CONSULAR CONVENTION BETWEEN JAPAN AND THE UNION OF SOVIET SOCIALIST REPUBLICS

Signed at Tokyo, July 29, 1966.

(Excerpt)

. . .

Article 32. 1. The competent authorities of the receiving state shall notify immediately the appropriate consular officer concerning the arrest or detention in other form of a national of the sending state.

2. A consular officer shall have the right without delay to visit with and to communicate with a national of the sending state who is under arrest or otherwise detained, or is serving a term of imprisonment. The rights specified in the present point shall be exercised in accordance with the laws and rules of the receiving state, on condition, however, that the said laws must not nullify these rights.

. . .

Protocol to the Consular Convention Between Japan and the Union of Soviet Socialist Republics

In signing the Consular Convention between Japan and the Union of Soviet Socialist Republics (further referred to as "Convention"), the Plenipotentiaries of the Contracting Parties who have signed below have agreed to the following provisions relating to application of the provisions of Article 32 of the Convention, which shall be an integral part of the Convention:

1. Notification of a consular officer of the arrest or detention in other form of a national of the sending state shall take place within one to three days (but not later) from the time of the arrest or detention depending on conditions of communication.

2. The rights of a consular officer to visit with and communicate with a national of the sending state who is under arrest or detention in other form shall be accorded within two to four days (but not later) from the time of the arrest or detention depending on the location of this national.

3. The rights of a consular officer to visit with and to communicate with a national of the sending state who is under arrest, detention in other form, or serving a term of imprisonment, shall be accorded on a periodic basis.

In witness thereof the Plenipotentiaries of both Contracting Parties have signed the present Protocol and have affixed their seals thereto.

Done in Tokyo on July 29, 1966, in two copies, each in the Japanese and Russian language, both texts being authentic.

Draft Letter of the Minister for Foreign Affairs of the USSR to the Japanese Minister for Foreign Affairs

Mister Minister:

Referring to the Protocol to the Consular Convention between the Union of Soviet Socialist Republics and Japan signed on the present date, I have the honor to confirm that the following agreement relating to the procedure for applying the provisions of the Protocol with respect to Japanese nationals arrested or detained by Soviet authorities for violation of the regime of territorial waters in the northwest part of the Pacific Ocean, including the Japan, Okhotsk, and Bering Seas, has been reached by our two Governments.

1. Notification of the consular section of the Embassy of Japan in the USSR of the arrest or detention in other form by Soviet authorities of Japanese nationals for violation of the regime of territorial waters in the northwest part of the Pacific Ocean shall take place in a period of up to ten days from the time of the arrest or detention.

2. a) A visit to a national by employees of the Embassy of Japan in the USSR who have been entrusted to fulfill consular functions specified in point 1 shall be carried out in each individual instance in accordance with an agreement between both parties reached through diplomatic channels.

b) The aforementioned employees may communicate with nationals specified in point 1 by letters and telegrams through ordinary means of communication.

3. None of the provisions of the present Letter must be considered as exerting any influence on the position of both Parties concerning questions of the breadth of territorial waters and their jurisdiction in the sphere of fishing.

I have the honor to propose that the present Letter* and the reply of Your Excellency confirming the aforesaid agreement be considered as the formulation of an agreement between the two Governments on the question concerned.

Accept, Mister Minister, assurances of my highest respect.

A. Gromyko
Minister for Foreign Affairs

Appendix 26

AGREEMENT ON FISHING BETWEEN THE GOVERNMENT OF THE UNION OF SOVIET SOCIALIST REPUBLICS AND THE GOVERNMENT OF THE KINGDOM OF NORWAY

Signed at Moscow, April 16, 1962. 437 UNTS 194.

The Government of the Union of Soviet Socialist Republics and the Government of the Kingdom of Norway,

Desiring to develop and strengthen good-neighborly relations between the two countries and to assure their common fishing interests in northern waters,

Have agreed as follows:

Article 1. For the purpose of this Agreement:

* (The draft reply of the Japanese Government, not translated, accepted the provisions of the letter above.)

(a) the term "mile" shall be understood to mean a nautical mile (1,852 meters).
(b) the term "vessel" shall be understood to mean any vessel or boat engaged in fishing.

Article 2. From the moment of the entry into force of this Agreement until October 31, 1970, the Government of the Kingdom of Norway shall permit fishing vessels registered in the Union of Soviet Socialist Republics and manned by Soviet nationals to fish in a Norwegian fishing zone between the limits of six and twelve miles from the base line from which the territorial waters of the Kingdom of Norway are measured.

However, in the areas indicated below, vessels of the Contracting Parties shall be limited to fishing with fixed nets and hand tackle:
(a) Andenes: from longitude 15°25' East to 16° East throughout the year;
(b) Vesteralen: from latitude 69°12' North to 69°18' North from May 16 to February 14, both dates inclusive;
(c) Grimsbakken: from latitude 69°43' North to 69°47' North from December 1 to April 15, both dates inclusive;
(d) Fugloybanken: from longitude 19° East to 19°30' East from December 1 to April 15, both dates inclusive.

Article 3. During the period indicated in Article 2 of this Agreement the Government of the Union of Soviet Socialist Republics shall permit fishing vessels registered in the Kingdom of Norway and manned by Norwegian nationals to engage in fishing in Soviet territorial waters in Varangerfjord between the limits of six and twelve miles from the shore in a zone bounded to the south by a line drawn along the Soviet coast six miles from the shore, to the south-east by a line drawn six miles from the base line from which Soviet territorial waters are measured running from the promontory at the entrance to the bay of Dolgaia Strait through the north-western extremity of the island of Bolshoi Ainov to Cape Nemetskii on Rybachy Peninsula, and to the north-east by a line joining Cape Nemetskii to Cape Kibergnes, as indicated on the map annexed to this Agreement.

Article 4. Fishing in the zones indicated in Articles 2 and 3 of this Agreement shall be carried on in accordance with the annexed Protocol, which is an integral part of the Agreement.

For purposes other than fishing, Norwegian nationals and vessels passing in Soviet territorial waters shall be subject to the laws and regulations of the Union of Soviet Socialist Republics relating to the presence in these waters of foreign nationals and vessels, without prejudice to the provisions of this Agreement.

Particulars of such laws and regulations and of amendments and additions thereto shall be notified to the Government of the Kingdom of Norway through the diplomatic channel.

Article 5. If at any time before October 31, 1970, either Contracting Party finds that there has been a radical change in the character of the fishing carried on by nationals of the other Party in the zones indicated in Articles 2 and 3 of this Agreement, the Government concerned may raise the matter with the Government of the other country and they shall together review the position.

Article 6. If in the zones indicated in Articles 2 and 3 of this Agreement fishing vessels belonging to fishermen of one Party should be damaged by the fault of fishermen of the other Party, claims for compensation shall be examined in accordance with the Agreement between the Government of the Union of Soviet Socialist Republics and the Norwegian Government of December 9, 1959, concerning the handling of claims in connection with damage to fishing gear.

Article 7. The Contracting Parties shall take the appropriate steps to ensure compliance with the provisions of this Agreement by their nationals and by vessels registered in their territories.

Article 8. This Agreement is subject to ratification. The exchange of the instruments of ratification shall take place as soon as possible, at Oslo, and the Agreement shall enter into force on the date of such exchange.

DONE in Moscow on April 16, 1962, in two copies, each in the Russian and Norwegian languages, both texts being equally authentic.

In Witness Whereof the undersigned, duly authorized thereto by their Governments, have signed this Agreement.

For the Government of the Union of Soviet Socialist Republics:

M. N. Sukhoruchenko

For the Government of the Kingdom of Norway:

Frithjof Jacobsen

PROTOCOL

RULES FOR THE REGULATION OF THE FISHERIES

Chapter I

Rules Concerning the Registration and Identification of Fishing Vessels

Article 1. 1. The vessels of each of the Contracting Parties shall be registered in accordance with the rules in force in the country of which they fly the flag.

2. The competent authorities of each of the Contracting Parties shall specify one or more initial letters and a consecutive series of numbers for the port of registration or for each maritime district.

3. The Contracting Parties shall communicate to one another a list of these identification marks and shall notify one another of all subsequent modifications thereto.

Article 2. 1. Every vessel shall bear, on the outside of the hull, clearly visible identification marks in the form of a letter or letters, the number under which the vessel is registered, the name of the port of registration, and the name of the vessel itself.

2. Small boats and all fishing implements shall be marked for identification purposes with a sufficiently clear and large letter or letters, and with the number of the vessel to which they belong. The ownership of nets or other fishing implements may be further distinguished by special marks.

3. The identification marks enumerated in paragraph 1 of this Article shall not be effaced, altered, made illegible or covered, nor shall the nationality of a vessel be concealed.

Article 3. 1. The master of each vessel shall have with him an official document issued by the competent authorities of his country, confirming the nationality of the vessel.

This document shall indicate the letter or letters and the number of the vessel, the name and nationality of the owner, or the name of the firm or company owning the vessel, and shall contain a precise description of the vessel.

2. Each vessel shall carry a ship's roll, drawn up by the competent authorities of the country concerned, showing the names, nationality and residence of all persons on board.

Article 4. Responsibility for ensuring that the provisions of Articles 1, 2 and 3 of the Protocol are complied with shall rest with the competent authorities of the country to which the vessel belongs. The commanders of fishery protection vessels of each Contracting Party shall inform each other of any violation of these provisions by vessels registered in the territory of the other Contracting Party.

Chapter II

Procedure Governing the Operation of Fishing

Article 5. Vessels arriving on fishing grounds where other vessels are already fishing or have set their gear for that purpose shall not place themselves or their fishing nets, buoys or other fishing implements in such a way as to interfere with or obstruct fishing operations already in progress.

Article 6. No vessel shall anchor or remain at anchor between sunset and sunrise in grounds where drift-net fishing is in progress during that period, except as a consequence of accident, shipwreck or other circumstances beyond the vessel's control.

Article 7. 1. Nets and lines anchored in the sea shall be furnished at each end with flag buoys by day and with light buoys by night. These buoys shall be clearly visible at a distance of at least two miles.

2. On fishing gear referred to in paragraph 1 of this Article extending for more than one mile, additional flag buoys or light buoys shall be placed at distances of not more than one mile from one another.

3. On fishing gear referred to in paragraph 1 of this Article which is attached to a vessel, a flag buoy or light buoy shall not be required at the end attached to the vessel.

Article 8. 1. Trawlers shall take all practicable steps to avoid anchored nets or buoys in order to prevent damage to them, and in particular to avoid trawling between two buoys.

2. No vessel shall make fast to or hold on to the nets, buoys, floats, or any other part of the fishing tackle of another vessel.

Article 9. Where it can be proved that damage has been caused to nets or lines by a trawler, the responsibility shall be presumed to lie with that trawler unless it proves:

(a) that the damage was done under circumstances beyond its control;

(b) that the damage was not due to its fault;

(c) that it had complied with the provisions of Articles 5, 6, 7 and 8 of this Protocol and had done all that was possible to avoid the damage, or

(d) that the vessel whose gear had been damaged had not complied with the provisions of Articles 5, 6, 7 and 8 of this Protocol, and that this circumstance had led to the damage.

Article 10. 1. When nets belonging to different vessels foul each other, they may not be severed without the consent of both parties unless it is impossible to disengage them by other means.

2. When vessels fishing with lines entangle their lines, the vessel which hauls up the lines shall not sever the lines of the other vessel unless they cannot be disengaged in any other way, in which case any lines which may be severed shall where possible be immediately joined together again.

3. Except in cases of salvage and the cases enumerated in paragraphs 1 and 2 of this Article, no vessel shall sever, hook or lift up fishing implements not belonging to it or damage them unnecessarily.

4. When a vessel fouls or otherwise interferes with gear not belonging to it, it shall take all measures to reduce to a minimum the damage to such gear which may result. The vessel to which the gear belongs shall at the same time avoid any action tending to aggravate such damage.

Article 11. All vessels, or their rigging, tackle and fishing implements or gear found or picked up at sea shall as soon as possible be delivered to the competent authorities in the first port in the territory of either Contracting Party to which the salvage vessel puts in.

Such authorities shall, where the circumstances permit, inform the consular representative of the country of which the owner of the salved property is a national. The property shall be restored to the owner or to his representative as soon as it has been claimed and the interests of the salving vessel have been properly guaranteed.

The amount of the reward to be paid to the salving vessel shall be determined by the authorities of the country in whose territory is situated the port in which the salved property was delivered.

Article 12. No vessel shall, except by reason of distress, dump in the sea fishing gear, appurtenances, or other articles which may obstruct or cause damage to fishing gear.

Chapter III

Procedure Relating to the Policing of the Fisheries

Article 13. 1. Responsibility for ensuring that the provisions of Chapter II of the Protocol are complied with in the zone referred to in Article 2 of the Agreement shall rest with the Norwegian fishery protection vessels.

2. Responsibility for ensuring that the provisions of Chapter II of the Protocol are complied with in the zone referred to in Article 3 of the Agreement shall rest with Soviet fishery protection vessels.

3. The commanders of vessels referred to in paragraphs 1 and 2 of this Article shall carry documentary proof of their right to superintend the conduct of fishing operations, such documents to be drawn up in Russian and Norwegian and to be issued by the competent authorities of the appropriate Contracting Party.

Article 14. 1. When the commander of a vessel referred to in paragraphs 1 and 2 of Article 13 has reason to believe that a vessel of the other Contracting Party has infringed the provisions of Chapter II of this Protocol, he or his representative may board the said vessel and search it, insofar as such search is necessary in order to find the required evidence.

The commander of a fishery protection vessel or his representative shall not remain longer on a vessel under search than is necessary for the conduct of the search.

Article 15. 1. When a vessel belonging to the other Contracting Party is being searched, the commander of the fishery protection vessel shall draw up a document, in Russian or Norwegian, of the reasons for and results of the search.

If, as a result of the search, the fact of an infringement by the fishing vessel of the provisions of Chapter II of this Protocol is established, the Contracting Party whose representatives have discovered the infringement shall notify the other Contracting Party accordingly.

2. The master of a fishing vessel accused of infringing the provisions of Chapter II of this Protocol, and the witnesses, shall be entitled to add observations to the statement, in their own language, and shall sign such observations.

EXCHANGE OF LETTERS

Moscow, February 22, 1962

Sir,

I have the honor to inform you herewith that the Government of the Union of Soviet Socialist Republics will permit fishing vessels registered in Norway and manned by Norwegian crews to engage in fishing in the territorial waters of the Soviet Union, in accordance with the provisions of the Soviet-Norwegian Agreement on Fishing initialled on February 22, 1962, at a distance of six to twelve miles from the shore in a zone bounded to the south-west by a straight line joining Cape Nemetskii to Cape Kibergnes, to the east by a marker passing through Cape Nemetskii, and to the south by a line drawn in an arc for a distance of eight miles from Cape Nemetskii, as shown on the map annexed to the said Agreement. The Government of the Soviet Union will grant the right to Norwegian nationals so long as Soviet vessels have the right to carry on loading and unloading operations connected with fishing in the region of Jan Mayen Island at a distance of four miles from the base line.*

(Signature)

* (The reply of the Norwegian Government accepted the terms contained in the letter above.)

Appendix 27

PROTOCOL BETWEEN THE GOVERNMENT OF THE POLISH PEOPLE'S REPUBLIC AND THE GOVERNMENT OF THE UNION OF SOVIET SOCIALIST REPUBLICS CONCERNING THE DELIMITATION OF POLISH AND SOVIET TERRITORIAL WATERS IN THE GULF OF GDANSK OF THE BALTIC SEA

Signed at Warsaw, March 18, 1958. 340 UNTS 94.

(Excerpt)

The Government of the Polish People's Republic and the Government of the Union of Soviet Socialist Republics,

Desiring to delimit Polish and Soviet territorial waters in the Gulf of Gdansk of the Baltic Sea and thus contribute to the strengthening of good-neighborly relations between the Polish People's Republic and the Union of Soviet Socialist Republics,

Have decided to conclude this Protocol to the Treaty of March 5, 1957, between the Polish People's Republic and the Union of Soviet Socialist Republics concerning the demarcation of the existing Polish-Soviet State frontier in the sector adjoining the Baltic Sea and have for that purpose appointed as their plenipotentiaries:

The Government of the Polish People's Republic:
Kazimierz Korolczyk, Deputy Departmental Director in the Ministry of Foreign Affairs;

The Government of the Union of Soviet Socialist Republics:
Dimitry Ivanovich Zaikin, Minister;

who, having exchanged their full powers, found in good and due form, have agreed on the following provisions:

Article 1. The boundary separating the territorial waters of the Polish People's Republic and the Union of Soviet Socialist Republics shall follow a line perpendicular to the shoreline at the terminal point of the Polish-Soviet State frontier on the Baltiiskaya Kosa (Mierzeja Wislana) and running to the point of intersection with the outer limit of the territorial waters of the Polish People's Republic. An extension of this line in the same direction to the point of intersection with the outer limit of the territorial waters of the Union of Soviet Socialist Republics shall constitute the boundary of the territorial waters of the Soviet Union.

. . .

Article 2. The Contracting Parties shall entrust all work relating to the delimitation of Polish and Soviet territorial waters in the Gulf of Gdansk of the Baltic Sea to the existing Mixed Polish-Soviet Commission for demarcation of the State frontier between the Polish People's Republic and the Union of Soviet Socialist Republics in the sector adjoining the Baltic Sea.

The Mixed Commission shall complete its work by August 1, 1958.

The expenses connected with these activities shall be shared equally between the Contracting Parties.

Article 3. This Protocol is subject to ratification and shall enter into force on the date of the exchange of the instruments of ratification.

The exchange of the instruments of ratification shall take place at Moscow as soon as possible.

DONE at Warsaw on March 18, 1958, in duplicate, in the Polish and Russian languages, both texts being equally authentic.

For the Government of the Polish People's Republic:	For the Government of the Union of Soviet Socialist Republics:
K. Korolczyk	D. Zaikin

C DIPLOMATIC CORRESPONDENCE

Appendix 28

EXCHANGE OF LETTERS BETWEEN THE PLENIPOTENTIARY REPRESENTATIVE OF THE USSR IN IRAN AND THE MINISTER OF FOREIGN AFFAIRS OF IRAN REGARDING THE CASPIAN SEA

10 SDD 71.

Letter of the Plenipotentiary Representative of the USSR in Iran Addressed to the Minister of Foreign Affairs of Iran of March 25, 1940

Mr. Minister,

I have the honor to bring to Your attention the following:

In view of the fact that the Caspian Sea, considered by both Contracting Parties as a Soviet and Iranian Sea, has exceptional interest for the Contracting Parties, it is established that both Governments shall take necessary measures so that nationals of third countries who are in the service of vessels of the respective Contracting Parties and in its ports on the Caspian Sea shall not use their service and presence on vessels and in ports for purposes exceeding the limits of the service duties placed upon them.

Please believe, Mr. Minister, that I have great respect for You.*

(Signature)

* The Iranian Ministry of Foreign Affairs confirmed the view of the Soviet representative in a reply dated the same day.

Appendix 29

EXCHANGE OF NOTES BETWEEN THE SOVIET UNION AND IRAN REGARDING THE OBLIGATION OF IRAN TO PREVENT THE CREATION OF FOREIGN MISSILE BASES ON ITS TERRITORY

September 15, 1962.

Note of the Iranian Ministry of Foreign Affairs

The Imperial Ministry of Foreign Affairs conveys its respect to the Embassy of the Union of Soviet Socialist Republics and, in the development of previous negotiations, considers it necessary to bring to the information of the Embassy that the Imperial Government desires by the present note to give to the Government of the Union of Soviet Socialist Republics a positive statement that it will not accord to any foreign state the right to have missile bases of any type on the territory of Iran, for the purposes of proclaiming its good will and strengthening the bases of friendship between the two countries.

Note of the Embassy of the USSR in Iran

The Embassy of the Union of Soviet Socialist Republics conveys its respect to the Imperial Ministry of Foreign Affairs of Iran and has the honor to declare that the Government of the USSR accepts with satisfaction the information in the note of the Imperial Government of Iran of September 15, 1962, which indicates that "The Imperial Ministry of Foreign Affairs conveys its respect to the Embassy of the Union of Soviet Socialist Republics and, in the development of previous negotiations, considers it necessary to bring to the information of the Embassy that the Imperial Government desires by the present note to give to the Government of the Union of Soviet Socialist Republics a positive statement that it will not accord to any foreign state the right to have missile bases of any type on the territory of Iran, for the purposes of proclaiming its good will and strengthening the bases of friendship between the two countries".

Statement of the Minister of Foreign Affairs of the Imperial Government of Iran in the Name of His Government, Made on September 15, 1962, Upon the Exchange of Notes

I officially declare that, as His Imperial Majesty the Shahinshah has more than once indicated, the Imperial Government of Iran shall never permit Iran to become a means of aggression against the territory of the Soviet Union.

Reciprocal Statement of the Ambassador of the USSR to Iran, Made Upon the Exchange of Notes

The Government of the Union of Soviet Socialist Republics takes due notice of the official statement of the Imperial Government of Iran concerning the fact that, as His Imperial Majesty the Shahinshah has more than once indicated, the Imperial Government of Iran shall never permit Iran to become a means of aggression against the territory of the Soviet Union. The Soviet Government expresses confidence that the said Statement of the Imperial Government, as well as the exchange of notes regarding the non-accordance to foreign states of the right to have missile bases of any type on the territory of Iran, serves to strengthen the bases of good-neighborly relations between the USSR and Iran and the interests of peace and security in the area of the Near and Middle East.

Appendix 30

NOTE OF THE PEOPLE'S COMMISSAR OF FOREIGN AFFAIRS OF THE RSFSR TO THE MINISTER OF FOREIGN AFFAIRS OF NORWAY, ILENA

May 4, 1920. 2 Dokumenty 500-501.

In addition to my radiogram of April 15th and to protests made by me on the occasion of arbitrary hunting in the northern waters of Russia, I have the honor to inform you that temporarily and up to and including a general resolution of the question pertaining to the extent of Russian territorial waters, the

Russian Government declares that it regards as Russian territorial waters in the north of Russia a zone of three nautical miles, computed from points and islands from the shore line at lowest ebb tide. As to the White Sea, inasmuch as the latter is an internal Russian sea, the aforementioned three-mile zone shall be calculated from a line drawn between Cape Sviatoi and Cape Kanin.

In transmitting the present communication to you, I consider it my duty to emphasize that the present decision of the Russian Government may in no way be cited in the future as depriving it of the right to adopt any other decree relating to the extent of Russian territorial waters in accordance with the political and economic interests of the country.

People's Commissar of Foreign Affairs
Chicherin

Appendix 31

TELEGRAM OF THE SOVIET COMMISSAR FOR FOREIGN AFFAIRS TO THE UNITED STATES SECRETARY OF STATE

December 11, 1924. 1924 _For. Rel. U.S.,_ Vol. 2, pp. 682-683.

Local Union authorities have delivered to Moscow a round brass mark discovered by them on Chukotsk Peninsula in Emma Bay, Cape Puzino. The said mark, set in a rock, bears the following inscription: "United States Coast and Geodetic Survey magnetic station. For information write to Superintendent, Washington. For disturbing this mark $250 fine or imprisonment." This mark, set up July 1920, shows magnetic observations had been carried out in aforementioned and subsequent years by the coastguard cruiser _Bear_ belonging to the United States Government. While pointing out that the repeated entry of an American war vessel into territorial waters of the Union Republics without permission is contrary to international law, I must emphasize that the setting up of the aforementioned mark and the threat to Soviet citizens borne by it constitute a gross violation of the sovereignty of the Soviet Republics. Emphatically protesting to the United States Government against such lawless acts of their officials, who were obviously unable to distinguish where their own state territory ends and other sovereign country's territory begins, I am obliged to notify that such violation of legitimate rights of the Union Republics, if repeated, will be sternly repressed by the Soviet Government.

Chicherin

D COURT DECISION

Appendix 32

CASE OF THE ST. HUBERT

March 8, 1922.

(Editor's Note: On March 23, 1922, the American Consul in Hull, England, transmitted to the United States Department of State a translation of a Soviet court decision relating to the seizure by Soviet authorities of the British steam trawler St. Hubert for violation of Russian fishing legislation. The following is an edited version of Consul Grout's communication. The original is to be found in the United States National Archives, File No. 361.4154Sa2/-.)

Final Declaration of the Soviet Court

On March 8, 1922, I, the examining Magistrate Ivanov, on special service at Sovnarousdya, Province of Sovnarousdya, to hear the case against George William Leighton, Master of the British trawler no. 493, in violation of a Decree adopted June 1, 1921, came to the conclusion:

THAT on February 20, 1922, Captain George William Leighton, of the British fishing trawler no. 493, the St. Hubert, sailed from the port of Hull under the orders of the St. Andrew Fishing Company on a fishing expedition near the area of the Lapland Islands.

This Company had warned Captain Leighton not to enter Russian waters (paragraph 10-11), whereas Captain Leighton was fishing in the area of the Lapland Islands and, having poor success, proceeded further and anchored 10 1/2 nautical miles from Cape Filiberka, i.e. in Russian waters, where he fished for three days (paragraph 10-11), and there was caught by Russian trawler no. 21 just at the moment when he was dropping into the sea the nets attached to the rigging hawser. He was brought into the Russian port of Murmansk in accordance with the Law on the Protection of Russian Waters.

. . .

The Master of the British trawler no. 493, George William Leighton, has been summoned by the Examining Magistrate and has been questioned; he has admitted that he was fishing in Russian waters; here he was told that the St. Andrew Fishing Company had warned him not to fish in Russian waters, but he did not take any notice, saying that he did not know of the Decree of the Commissar of the Soviet Government dated June 1, 1921. Captain Leighton knew only the law of the three-mile limit. (Captain Leighton was prosecuted under the Decree Concerning Protection of Fisheries and Furbearing Animals in the Northern Arctic Ocean and the White Sea of May 24, 1921, SU RSFSR (1921), no. 49, item 259.--Ed.)

Taking into consideration that Captain Leighton was warned by the St. Andrew Fishing Company not to fish in Russian waters, the excuse of Captain Leighton that he did not know of the Decree of the Commissar of the Soviet Government dated June 1, 1921, has not been accepted by us.

By virtue of the above facts, I found it necessary to put the case in the hands of the People's Court, First Murmansk Province, Captain of the British fishing trawler no. 493, George William Leighton, 47 years of age, resident of Hull (United Kingdom) having been found guilty as follows:

That on February 20, 1922, he sailed on British fishing trawler no. 493 on a fishing expedition by request of the St. Andrew Fishing Company to the Lapland Islands, although having received orders from St. Andrew Fishing Company not to fish in Russian waters. He did ignore the orders and by so doing he violated the Decree of the Commissar of the Soviet Government dated June 1, 1921.

. . .

SELECTED BIBLIOGRAPHY

This is a selected bibliography, consisting of books, articles, and reviews cited in the text or those found to be particularly useful by the author as supplemental sources or collateral reading. The emphasis is obviously on Russian language materials not as well known as the standard Western treatments. Many are exceedingly difficult to obtain; several are not to be found in American libraries.

In a work as specialized as this one, it did not seem necessary to break down the bibliography into subcategories.

The best list, but not without inaccuracies and omissions, of Soviet treaties and legislation from 1917-54 pertaining to Soviet territorial waters will be found in A. N. Nikolaev's book. It also was reproduced and updated to 1957 by Hartingh. Relevant documents from 1957-1966 are cited in the notes of this book.

Admiralty Naval Staff, Intelligence Division, _A Handbook of Siberia and Arctic Russia_ (London: His Majesty's Stationary Office, 1920).

Aleksandrov, B. A., "Pravo rybolovstva v territorialnykh vodakh v zakonodatelstve i mezhdunarodnykh dogovorakh soiuza SSR," (Right of Fishing in Territorial Waters in Legislation and International Treaties of the USSR), _Mezhdunarodnaia zhizn_, no. 9-10 (1928), p. 94-99.

Armstrong, Terence, _The Northern Sea Route: Soviet Exploitation of the North East Passage_ (New York, 1952).

Avsov, Iu. A., Egorev, V. V., Keilin, A. D., _Morskoe pravo SSSR_ (_Maritime Law of the USSR_) (Moscow-Leningrad: Vneshtorgizdat, 1932).

Bakhov, A. S., _Voenno-morskoi mezhdunarodno-pravovoi spravochnik_ (_Naval International Law Manual_) (Moscow: Voengiz, 1956).

Barabolia, P. D., Ivanashchenko, L. A., Kolesnik, D. N., Mezhdunarodno-pravovoi rezhim vazhneishikh prolivov i kanalov (International Legal Regime of the Most Important Straits and Canals), (Moscow: Gosiurizdat, 1965).

Barabolia, P. D., et. al., Voenno-morskoi mezhdunarodno-pravovoi spravochnik (Naval International Law Manual) (Moscow: Voenizdat, 1966).

Barnes, Kathleen, "Fisheries: Mainstay of Soviet-Japanese Friction," Far Eastern Survey, Vol. 9 (1940), p. 75-80.

Belli, V. A., Voenno-morskoi mezhdunarodno-pravovoi spravochnik (Naval International Law Manual) (Moscow-Leningrad: NKVMF, 1939-1940).

Berman, Harold J., Justice in the U.S.S.R. (Cambridge: Harvard University Press, rev. ed., 1963).

Berman, Harold J., intro., Soviet Criminal Law and Procedure: The RSFSR Codes (Cambridge: Harvard University Press, 1966). (Translation by H. J. Berman and J. W. Spindler).

Bilmanis, Alfred, The Baltic States and the Problem of Freedom of the Baltic Sea (Washington, D. C., 1943).

Bohmert, Viktor, "Die russische Fischereigrenze," Zeitschrift fur Volkerrecht, Vol. 21 (1937), p. 441-496; (1938), p. 257-306.

Borisov, S., "Mezhdunarodnyi sud o territorialnykh vodakh," (The International Court on Territorial Waters), Sovetskoe gosudarstvo i pravo, no. 8 (1952), p. 52-54.

Bouchez, Leo J., The Regime of Bays in International Law (Leyden: Sijthoff, 1964).

Bowett, D. W., The Law of the Sea (New York: Oceana Publications, 1967).

Butler, William E., trans. and ed., Customs Code of the USSR (Washington, D. C.: Hazen Publications, 1966).

Butler, William E., "Soviet Concepts of Innocent Passage," Harvard International Law Journal, Vol. 7 (1965), p. 113-130.

Butler, William E., Berman, Harold J., trans., "Soviet International Law: Legal Status of Foreigners in the USSR," Soviet Statutes and Decisions, Vol. 3, no. 1 (1966), p. 55-59.

Butler, William E., "Soviet Territorial Waters," World Affairs, Vol. 130 (1967), p. 17-25.

Butler, William E., Writings on Soviet Law and Soviet International Law: A Bibliography of Books and Articles Published Since 1917 in Languages Other Than East European (Cambridge: Harvard Law School Library, 1966).

Cherepakhin, B., "Der Schleppvertrag im See- und Binnenschiffahrtsrecht der Sovetunion," Zeitschrift fur Ostrecht, Vol. 5 (1931), p. 689-699.

Colombos, C. J., The International Law of the Sea (London: Longmans, 5th ed., 1962).

Cooper, Denis A., The Air Code of the U.S.S.R. (Charlottesville: Michie, 1966).

Dobrin, Samuel, "Apropos the Soviet Maritime Code," Law Quarterly Review, Vol. 49 (1933), p. 249-267.

Dobrin, Samuel, "The Soviet Maritime Code, 1929," Journal of Comparative Legislation, Vol. 16 (1934), p. 252-268.

Dranov, B. A., Chernomorskie prolivy: mezhdunarodno-pravovoi rezhim (The Black Sea Straits: International Legal Regime) (Moscow: Iurizdat, 1948).

Durdenevskii, V. N., Vereshchetin, V. S., "Frantsuzskii mezhdunarodnik o sovetskoi kontseptsii morskogo prava," (A French International Jurist on the Soviet Concept of Maritime Law), Sovetskoe gosudarstvo i pravo, no. 10 (1960), p. 134-135.

Durdenevskii, V. N., Krylov, S. B., ed., Mezhdunarodnoe pravo (International Law) (Moscow: Iurizdat, 1947).

Durdenevskii, V. N., ed., Mezhdunarodnoe pravo v izbrannykh dokumentakh (International Law in Selected Documents), (Moscow: izd-vo IMO, 1957). 3 Vols.

Egorev, V. V., "Gaagskaia konferentsiia po territorialnym vodam," (The Hague Conference on Territorial Waters), Morskoi sbornik, no. 7 (1930), p. 80-91.

Egorov, K. F., Shmigelskii, G. L., Pravovye voprosy okazaniia pomoshchi i spasaniia na more (Legal Problems of Rendering Aid and Rescue at Sea) (Moscow: izd-vo Morskoi transport, 1961).

Egorov, V., "Novyi dogovornyi rezhim v finskogo zaliva," (New Treaty Regime in the Gulf of Finland), Mezhdunarodnaia zhizn, no. 11 (1929), p. 102-109.

Freund, Heinrich, Das Seeschiffahrtsrecht der Sowjetunion (Stuttgart, 1930).

Fulton, T. A., The Sovereignty of the Sea (Edinburgh, 1911).

Ginsburgs, George, Shrewsbury, Scott, "The Soviet-Japanese Fisheries Problem in the North-West Pacific," International Studies, Vol. 5 (1964), p. 259-280.

Glazer, E., "O roli odnostoronnogo akta pribrezhnogo gosudarstva v ustanovlenii shiriny territorialnykh vod," (On the Role of a Unilateral Act of a Littoral State in Establishing the Breadth of Territorial Waters), in Problemy mezhdunarodnogo prava (Moscow: izd-vo IL, 1961), p. 217-265.

Glenn, Gene, "The Swedish-Soviet Territorial Sea Controversy in the Baltic," American Journal of International Law, Vol. 50 (1956), p. 942-949.

Golder, F. A., Russian Expansion on the Pacific 1641-1850 (Gloucester, Mass.: Peter Smith, 1960), p. 250-266. (Reprint ed.)

Golubev, A., "More territorialnoe i zakrytoe," (Territorial and Closed Sea), Torgovyi flot, no. 1 (1926), p. 29-31.

Golubev, V., "Primenenie mezhdunarodnykh obychaev i prava v oblasti morskogo prava RSFSR," (Application of International Customs and Law in the Area of Maritime Law of the RSFSR), Sovetskoe pravo, no. 2 (1923), p. 56-64.

Grabar, V. E., Materialy k istorii literatury mezhdunarodnogo prava v rossii (Materials For a History of International Law in Russia) (Moscow: izd-vo Akademiia nauk SSSR, 1958).

Gray, Whitmore, ed., Soviet Civil Legislation (Ann Arbor: University of Michigan Law School, 1965).

Grzybowski, Kazimierz, Soviet Private International Law (Leyden: Sijthoff, 1965).

Grzybowski, Kazimierz, The Socialist Commonwealth of Nations: Organizations and Institutions (New Haven: Yale University Press, 1964).

Grzybowski, Kazimierz, "The Soviet Doctrine of Mare Clausum and Policies in Black and Baltic Seas," Journal of Central European Affairs, Vol. 14 (1955), p. 339-353.

Harben, William N., "Soviet Positions Concerning Maritime Waters," JAG Journal, Vol. 15 (1961), p. 149-154, 160.

Harbron, John D., Communist Ships and Shipping (New York: Frederick A. Praeger, 1963).

Hartingh, France de, Les Conceptions Sovietiques du Droit de la Mer (Paris: Pichon, 1960).

Harvard Law School Library, Soviet Legal Bibliography: A classified and annotated listing of books and serials published in the Soviet Union since 1917 as represented in the collection of the Harvard Law School Library as of January 1, 1965 (Cambridge: Harvard Law School, 1965). (Compiled by Vaclav Mostecky and William E. Butler).

Hazard, John N., Law and Social Change in the U.S.S.R. (London: Stevens & Sons, 1953).

Hurewitz, J., "Russia and the Turkish Straits: A Reevaluation of the Origins of the Problem," World Politics, Vol. 14 (1962), p. 605-632.

Imenitov, G. I., Sovetskoe morskoe i rybolovnoe pravo (Soviet Maritime and Fishing Law) (Moscow: Gosiurizdat, 1951).

Irie, Keishiro, "Status of Peter the Great Bay," Law Journal, Vol. 28, no. 9 (1956), p. 102-103. (In Japanese)

Ivanashchenko, L. A., "Mezhdunarodnaia konferentsiia po morskomu pravu," (International Conference on the Law of the Sea), Morskoi sbornik, no. 5 (1959), p. 67-79.

Ivanov, F., "Chetvertaia sessiia komissii mezhdunarodnogo prava OON," (Fourth Session of the UN International Law Commission), Sovetskoe gosudarstvo i pravo, no. 11 (1952), p. 72-79.

Jessup, Philip C., The Law of Territorial Waters and Maritime Jurisdiction (New York: Jennings, 1927).

Jessup, Philip C., "The United Nations Conference on the Law of the Sea," Columbia Law Review, Vol. 59 (1959), p.234-268.

Kamarovskii, L. A., Ulianitskii, V. A., Mezhdunarodnoe pravo po lektsiiam (International Law Lectures) (Moscow, 1908).

Kawakami, Kenzo, "Outline of the Japanese-Soviet Fishery Talks," Japanese Annual of International Law, Vol. 7 (1963), p. 24-29.

Kazanskii, P. E., Uchebnik mezhdunarodnogo prava (Textbook of International Law) (Odessa, 1902).

Keilin, A. D., "Der Seefrachtvertrag nach dem Seerecht der Sovetunion," Zeitschrift fur Ostrecht, Vol. 3 (1929), p. 193-227.

Keilin, A. D., "Die Grundlagen des Seerechts der Sovetunion," Zeitschrift fur Ostrecht, Vol. 1 (1927), p. 1-34.

Keilin, A. D., "Le Droit Maritime de l'Union Sovietique," Le Droit Maritime Francais, Vol. 11 (1959), p. 628-631.

Keilin, A. D., Vinogradov, P. P., Morskoe pravo (Maritime Law) (Moscow: izd-vo Morskoi transport, 1939).

Keilin, A. D., "Problemy rybolovstva v mezhdunarodnykh otnosheniiakh," (Problems of Fishing in International Relations), Vneshniaia torgovlia, no. 10 (1944), p.28-34.

Keilin, A. D., Sovetskoe morskoe pravo (Soviet Maritime Law) (Moscow: izd-vo Vodnogo transporta, 1954).

Keishiro, Irie, "The Synopsis of the Russo-Japanese Fishery Pact," Foreign Affairs Quarterly, Vol. 1, no. 1 (1956), p. 37-43. (In Japanese)

Kent, H. S. K., "The Historical Origins of the Three Mile Limit," American Journal of International Law, Vol. 48 (1954), p. 537-553.

Kerner, Robert J., The Urge to the Sea: The Course of Russian History (Berkeley: University of California Press, 1946).

Kiralfy, A. K. R., The Civil Code and the Code of Civil Procedure of the RSFSR 1964 (Leyden: Sijthoff, 1966).

Kodeks torgovogo moreplavaniia soiuza SSR (Merchant Shipping Code of the USSR) (Moscow: izd-vo Morskoi transport, 1953 and 1958 ed.).

Kolodkin, A. L., Pravovoi rezhim territorialnykh vod i otkrytogo moria (Legal Regime of Territorial Waters and the High Seas) (Moscow: izd-vo Morskoi transport, 1961).

Koretskii, V. M., Tunkin, G. I., ed., Ocherki mezhdunarodnogo morskogo prava (Outlines of International Maritime Law) (Moscow: Gosiurizdat, 1962).

Korovin, E. A., ed., Mezhdunarodnoe pravo (International Law), (Moscow: Gosiurizdat, 1951).

Korovin, E. A., "SSSR i poliarnye zemli," (The USSR and Polar Lands), Sovetskoe pravo, no. 3 (1926), p. 46.

Korovin, E. A., "U. S. Violation of the Principle of Freedom of the Seas," International Affairs, no. 3 (1955), p. 57-65.

Kozhevnikov, F. I., ed., International Law (Moscow: Foreign Languages Publishing House, 1961).

Kozhevnikov, F. I., ed., Kurs mezhdunarodnogo prava (Textbook of International Law), (Moscow: izd-vo IMO, 1966).

Kozhevnikov, F. I., ed., Mezhdunarodnoe pravo (International Law), (Moscow: Gosiurizdat, 1957).

Kozhevnikov, F. I., ed., Mezhdunarodnoe pravo (International Law), (Moscow: izd-vo IMO, 1964).

Krylov, S. B., "Angliia i vopros o shirine territorialnykh vod (pismo k redaktsiiu)," (England and the Question of the Breadth of Territorial Waters: Letter to the Editor), Sovetskoe gosudarstvo i pravo, no. 3 (1959), p. 125.

Krypton, Constantine, The Northern Sea Route and the Economy of the Soviet North (New York: Frederick A. Praeger, 1956).

Kucherov, Samuel A., "Das Problem der Kustenmeere und die Sowjetunion," Osteuropa Recht, Vol. 5 (1959), p. 15-24.

Lakhtin, V. L., Prava na severnye poliarnye prostranstva (Rights in Northern Polar Expanses) (Moscow: Litizdat NKID, 1928).

Lakhtin, V. L., "Prava soiuza SSSR v arktike," (Rights of the USSR in the Arctic), Rabochii sud, no. 15 (1928), p. 1135-1144.

Lakhtin, V. L., "Rights Over the Arctic," American Journal of International Law, Vol. 24 (1930), p. 703-717.

Lapenna, Ivo, Conceptions Sovietiques de Droit International Public (Paris: Pedone, 1954).

Lashkevich, G., "K voprosu o territorialnom more," (On the Question of the Territorial Sea), Mezhdunarodnaia zhizn, no. 1-2 (1923), p. 25-34.

Levin, D. B., Kaliuzhnaia, G. P., Mezhdunarodnoe pravo (International Law), (Moscow: Gosiurizdat, 1960; 2d ed., 1964).

Lisovskii, V. I., Mezhdunarodnoe pravo (International Law) (Kiev: Kievskii universitet, 1955; 2d ed., 1961).

Lissitzyn, Oliver J., International Law Today and Tomorrow (New York: Oceana, 1965).

Malinin, S. A., "K voprosu o pravovoi klassifikatsii vodnykh prostranstv," (On the Question of the Legal Classification of Water Expanses), Informatsionnyi sbornik, vyp. 46, no. 8 (Leningrad: 1960), p. 13-19.

Mandelstam, Andre N., "La Politique Russe d' Acces a la Mediterrainee au XX Siecle," Recueil des Cours, Vol. 47 (1934), p. 602-801.

Manzhin, V. V., comp., Sbornik zakonov i rasporiazhenii po torgovomu moreplavaniiu i portam (Collected Laws and Regulations Relating to Commercial Navigation and Ports) (Moscow: izd-vo Morskoi transport, 1940).

Martens, F. F., Sovremennoe mezhdunarodnoe pravo tsvilizovannykh narodov (Contemporary International Law of Civilized Peoples) (St. Petersburg: 1904).

Martin, L. W., The Sea in Modern Strategy (New York: Frederick A. Praeger, 1967).

Masterson, William E., Jurisdiction in Marginal Seas (New York: Macmillan, 1929).

Mateesco, Mircea, Le Droit Maritime Sovietique face au Droit Occidental (Paris: Pedone, 1966).

Mayeda, M., "The Russo-Japanese Dispute on Fishing Rights," Journal of International Law and Diplomacy, Vol. 29, no. 9 (1930), p. 10. (In Japanese)

Meijer, C. B. V., The Extent of Jurisdiction in Coastal Waters (Leyden: Sijthoff, 1937).

Meissner, Boris, intro., Sowjetunion und Volkerrecht 1917 bis 1962: Eine bibliographische Dokumentation (Koln: Verlag Wissenschaft und Politik, 1963).

Mellor, Roy E. H., Geography of the U.S.S.R. (New York: St. Martin's, 1964).

Meshera, V. F., Immunitet gosudarstvennykh morskikh sudov SSSR (Immunity of State Sea-Going Vessels of the USSR) (Moscow-Leningrad: izd-vo Morskoi transport, 1950).

Meshera, V. F., Morskoe pravo (Maritime Law) (Moscow: izd-vo Morskoi transport, 1958-1959). 3 Vols.

Meshera, V. F., "Problema kodifikatsii sovetskogo morskogo prava," (The Problem of Codification of Soviet Maritime Law), Uchenye zapiski, vyp. 7 (Leningrad, 1957).

Mezhdunarodnye konventsii i soglasheniia, otnosiashchiesia k torgovomu moreplavaniiu (International Conventions and Agreements Relating to Commercial Navigation) (Moscow: izd-vo Morskoi transport, 1940).

Mikhailov, V. S., "Mezhdunarodno-pravovoe regulirovanie rybolovstva i drugikh morskikh promyslov na tikhom okeane," (International Legal Regulation of Fishing and Other Maritime Trades in the Pacific Ocean), Sovetskii ezhegodnik mezhdunarodnogo prava 1960 (Moscow: izd-vo AN SSSR, 1961), p. 189-205.

Mitchell, Mairin, The Maritime History of Russia 848-1948 (London: Sidgwick & Jackson, 1949).

Molodtsov, S. V., "Kodifikatsiia i dalneishee razvitie mezhdunarodnogo morskogo prava," (Codification and Further Development of International Maritime Law), Sovetskii ezhegodnik mezhdunarodnogo prava 1958 (Moscow: izd-vo AN SSSR, 1959), p. 327-345.

Molodtsov, S. V., Mezhdunarodno-pravovoi rezhim baltiiskikh prolivov (International Legal Regime of the Baltic Straits) (Moscow, 1949). (dissertation)

Molodtsov, S. V., Mezhdunarodno-pravovoi rezhim otkrytogo moria i kontinentalnogo shelfa (International Legal Regime of the High Seas and Continental Shelf) (Moscow: izd-vo Akademiia nauk, 1960).

Molodtsov, S. V., "Nekotorye voprosy regulirovaniia pravogo rezhima otkrytogo moria," (Some Questions of the Regulation of the Legal Regime of the High Seas), Sovetskii ezhegodnik mezhdunarodnogo prava 1959 (Moscow: izd-vo AN SSSR, 1960), p. 327-341.

Movchanovskii, B. F., Orlov, V. A., Ocherki sovetskogo morskogo prava (Outlines of Soviet Maritime Law) (Moscow: Gostransizdat, 1931).

Nikolaev, A. N., "Obsuzhdenie voprosy territorialnykh vod," (Discussion of the Question of Territorial Waters), Morskoi flot, no. 8 (1958), p. 26-28.

Nikolaev, A. N., "O zalive Petra Velikogo," (On Peter the Great Bay), Mezhdunarodnaia zhizn, no. 2 (1958), p. 50-57.

Nikolaev, A. N., Problema territorialnykh vod v mezhdunarodnom prave (The Problem of Territorial Waters in International Law) (Moscow: Gosiurizdat, 1954).

Ohira, Zengo, "Fishery Problems Between Soviet Russia and Japan," Japanese Annual of International Law, Vol. 2 (1958), p. 1-19.

Orlenko, P. P., Ivanashchenko, L. A., Mezhdunarodnoe morskoe pravo (International Maritime Law) (Moscow, 1955).

Pashukanis, E. B., Ocherki po mezhdunarodnomu pravu (Outlines of International Law) (Moscow: izd-vo Sovetskoe zakonodatelstvo, 1935).

Petrow, Richard, Across the Top of Russia: The Cruise of the USCGC Northwind into the Polar Seas North of Siberia (New York: David McKay, 1967).

Pundeff, Martin, "Bulgarian Decree on Territorial Waters," American Journal of International Law, Vol. 46 (1952), p. 330-.

Ramundo, Bernard A., Peaceful Coexistence: International Law in the Building of Communism (Baltimore: Johns Hopkins Press, 1967).

Rautenkranz, Helmuth, Die Volkerrechtliche Ordnung des Verkehrs in der Ostsee (Leipzig, 1934).

Reinkemeyer, H. A., Die sowjetische Zwolfmeilenzone in der Ostsee und die Freiheit des Meeres (Koln: Heymann, 1955).

Romanov, V., "Zaliv Petra Velikogo - vnutrennie vody sovetskogo soiuza," (Peter the Great Bay - Internal Waters of the Soviet Union), Sovetskoe gosudarstvo i pravo, no. 5 (1958), p. 47-55.

Rykachev, V. N., Morskoe torgovoe pravo: sravnitelnyi sistematicheskii ocherk zakonodatelstva SSSR, anglii, germanii i frantsii (Commercial Maritime Law: Comparative Systematic Outline of Soviet, English, German, and French Legislation) (Moscow: izd-vo Transpechat, 1928).

Rzepka, Walter, "Grundzuge des sowjetischen Wasserrechts," Recht in Ost und West, Vol. 6 (1962), p. 189-195.

Sbornik rasporiazhenii po morskomu transportu (Collected Regulations Pertaining to Maritime Transport) (Moscow: izd-vo Transpechat, 1923).

Schapiro, Leonard B., Soviet Treaty Series: A Collection of Bilateral Treaties, Agreements, Conventions, Etc., Concluded Between the Soviet Union and Foreign Powers, 1917-1939 (Washington D. C.: Georgetown University Press, 1950-1955).

Schapiro, Leonard B., "The Limits of Russian Territorial Waters in the Baltic," British Yearbook of International Law, Vol. 27 (1950), p. 439-448.

Schweder, H., Russland und die Ostsee (Riga, 1927).

Semyonov, Yuri, Siberia: Its Conquest and Development (Baltimore: Helicon Press, 1963).

Sheptovitskii, M. Ia., Morskoe pravo (Maritime Law) (Leningrad: Gostransizdat, 1936).

Shmigelskii, G. L., Iasinovskii, V. A., Osnovy sovetskogo morskogo prava (Fundamental Principles of Soviet Maritime Law) (Moscow: izd-vo Morskoi transport, 1959; 2d ed., 1963).

Sigrist, S. V., "Sovetskoe pravo v poliarnykh prostranstvakh," (Soviet Law in the Polar Expanses), Rabochii sud, no. 13 (1928), p. 982-987.

Siling, A. N., Morskoe pravo (Maritime Law) (Moscow: izd-vo Transport, 1964).

Siling, A. N., Narusheniia imperialisticheskimi gosudarstvami svobody moreplavaniia i rybolovstva v otkrytom more (Violations by Imperialist States of Freedom of Navigation and Fishing on the High Seas) (Moscow: Gosiurizdat, 1963).

Sivers, V., Glavneishie svedeniia po morskomu mezhdunarodnomu pravu (Most Important Information Concerning International Maritime Law) (St. Petersburg, 1902).

Slusser, Robert M., Triska, Jan F., A Calendar of Soviet Treaties (Stanford: Hoover Institution, 1959); updated annually in Osteuropa Recht.

Smith, H. A., ed., Great Britain and the Law of Nations: A Selection of Documents Illustrating the Views of the Government of the United Kingdom Upon Matters of International Law (2 Vols., London, 1932-1935).

Sobakin, V. K., comp., Sovremennoe mezhdunarodnoe pravo:

sbornik dokumentov (Contemporary International Law: Collected Documents), (Moscow: izd-vo IMO, 1964).

Sorenson, Max, "Law of the Sea," International Conciliation, No. 520 (November 1958).

Spirin, V. G., "Problema territorialnykh vod v praktike latino-amerikanskikh stran," (Problem of Territorial Waters in the Practice of Latin American Countries), Sovetskoe gosudarstvo i pravo, no. 7 (1956), p. 118-122.

Strohl, Mitchell P., The International Law of Bays (The Hague: Nijhoff, 1963), p. 332-367.

Sugiyama, Shigeo, "The Japanese-Soviet Tangle Collection Agreement of 1963," Japanese Annual of International Law, Vol. 8 (1964), p. 75-98.

Sumner, B. H., A Short History of Russia (New York: Harcourt Brace, 1949).

Szirmai, Zsolt, Korevaar, J. D., trans., The Merchant Shipping Code of the Soviet Union (Leyden: Sijthoff, 1960).

Taracouzio, T. A., The Soviet Union and International Law (New York: Macmillan, 1935), p. 60-69.

Thommen, T. K., Legal Status of Government Merchant Ships in International Law (The Hague: Nijhoff, 1962).

Tunkin, G. I., Ideologicheskaia borba i mezhdunarodnoe pravo (Ideological Struggle and International Law) (Moscow: izd-vo IMO, 1967).

Tunkin, G.I., Voprosy teorii mezhdunarodnogo prava (Questions of the Theory of International Law) (Moscow: Gosiurizdat, 1962).

Tunkin, G. I., "Zhenevskaia konferentsiia po mezhdunarodnomu morskomu pravu," (The Geneva Conference on the Law of the Sea), Mezhdunarodnaia zhizn, no. 7 (1958), p. 63-70.

Uchida, Hisashi, "On the Soviet Theory of Territorial Waters,"

Journal of International Law and Diplomacy, Vol. 56 (1957), p. 151-180. (In Japanese)

Ulianitskii, V. A., Mezhdunarodnoe pravo (International Law) (Tomsk, 1911).

USSR Ministry of Foreign Affairs, Dokumenty vneshnei politiki SSSR (Documents on USSR Foreign Policy), (Moscow: Gospolitizdat, 1957-). 12 Vols.

USSR Ministry of Foreign Affairs, Sbornik deistvuiushchikh dogovorov, soglashenii, i konventsii, zakliuchennykh SSSR s inostrannymi gosudarstvami (Collected Treaties, Agreements, and Conventions in Force, Concluded by the USSR with Foreign States) (Moscow: Gospolitizdat, v.d.).20 Vols.

USSR Ministry of the Merchant Marine, Mezhdunarodnye konventsii i soglasheniia, otnosiashchiesia k torgovomu moreplavaniiu (International Conventions and Agreements Relating to Commercial Navigation) (Moscow-Leningrad: izd-vo Morskoi transport, 1951).

USSR Naval Hydrographic Office, Izveshcheniia moreplavateliam (Notices to Mariners) (Leningrad: weekly publication).

United Nations, Yearbook of the International Law Commission (New York: United Nations, 1954-1958).

United Nations Conference on the Law of the Sea, Geneva, 1958, Official Records (London: United Nations, 1958).

United Nations Conference on the Law of the Sea, 2d, Geneva, 1960, Official Records (New York: United Nations, 1962).

United Nations Legislative Series, Laws and Regulations on the Regime of the High Seas (New York: United Nations, 1951-1952), p. 116-130; Vol. 2, p. 121.

United Nations Legislative Series, Laws and Regulations on the Regime of the Territorial Sea (New York: United Nations, 1957), p. 45, 255-272, 577-578.

United Nations Legislative Series, Laws Concerning the

Nationality of Ships (New York: United Nations, 1955), p. 176-180.

United States Department of State, Sovereignty of the Sea (Washington, D.C.: GPO, 1965) (Geographic Bulletin No. 3).

United States Naval Oceanographic Office, Navigation Dictionary (Washington, D.C.: GPO, 1963 ed.).

United States Naval Oceanographic Office, Sailing Directions for East Coast of Siberia (Washington, D.C.: GPO, 1954 and supp.).

United States Naval Oceanographic Office, Sailing Directions for Northern U.S.S.R. (Washington, D.C.: GPO, 1954 and supp.).

United States Naval Oceanographic Office, Sailing Directions for the Baltic (Washington, D.C.: GPO, 1958 and supp.).

Uschakow, Alexander, intro., Das sowjetische Internationale Privatrecht 1917 bis 1962: Eine bibliographische Dokumentation (Koln: Verlag Wissenschaft und Politik, 1964).

Uustal, A. T., "Iskhodnaia liniia territorialnykh vod," (Baseline of Territorial Waters), Uchenye zapiski tartuskogo universiteta, Vyp. 61 (1959), p. 25-46.

Uustal, A. T., Mezhdunarodno-pravovoi rezhim territorialnykh vod (International Legal Regime of Territorial Waters) (Tartu: Tartuskii universitet, 1958).

Uustal, A. T., "Osnovnye voprosy pravovogo rezhima territorialnykh vod," (Basic Questions of the Legal Regime of Territorial Waters), Sovetskoe gosudarstvo i pravo, no. 6 (1957), p. 71-79.

Vasilev, I., O turetskom "neitralitete" vo vremia vtoroi mirovoi voiny (On Turkish "Neutrality" During World War II) (Moscow: Gospolitizdat, 1951).

Vereshchetin, V. S., "K voprosu o territorialnykh vodakh," (On the Question of Territorial Waters), Mirovaia ekonomika i mezhdunarodnye otnosheniia, no. 12 (1958), p. 117-119.

Vereshchetin, V. S., Svoboda sudokhodstva v otkrytom more (Freedom of Navigation on the High Seas) (Moscow: izd-vo IMO, 1958).

Volkov, A. A., "Pravovoi rezhim rybolovnykh zon," (Legal Regime of Fishing Zones), Sovetskii ezhegodnik mezhdunarodnogo prava 1963 (Moscow: izd-vo Nauka, 1965), p. 204-218.

Volkov, A. A., Sbornik mezhdunarodnykh konventsii, dogovorov, i soglashenii o rybolovstve i rybokhoziaistvennykh issledovaniiakh (Collected International Conventions, Treaties and Agreements Concerning Fishing and Fishery Conservation Research) (Moscow, 1961).

Vyshnepolskii, S. A., "Freedom of the Seas in the Epoch of Imperialism," Current Digest of the Soviet Press, Vol. 1, no. 16 (1949), p. 3-12.

Vyshnepolskii, S. A., "K probleme pravogo rezhim arkticheskoi oblasti," (On the Problem of the Legal Regime of the Arctic Region), Sovetskoe gosudarstvo i pravo, no. 7 (1952), p. 36-.

Vyshnepolskii, S. A., Mirovye morskie puti i sudokhodstvo (World Maritime Routes and Navigation) (Moscow: Geografgiz, 1953).

Wertheim, Barbara, "The Russo-Japanese Fisheries Controversy," Pacific Affairs, Vol. 8 (1935), p. 185-198.

Zakharov, N.A., Kurs obshchago mezhdunarodnogo prava (Course of General International Law) (Petrograd, 1918).

Zhudro, A. K., et. al., Morskoe pravo (Maritime Law) (Moscow, 1964).

Zhudro, A. K., Pravovoe regulirovanie deiatelnosti morskikh torgovykh portov SSSR. (Legal Regulation of the Activities of Commercial Sea Ports of the USSR) (Moscow: izd-vo Morskoi transport, 1957).

Zhudro, A. K., "Zhenevskaia konferentsiia OON po mezhdunarodnomu morskomu pravu," (UN Geneva Conference on the Law of the Sea), Informatsionnyi sbornik, vyp. 34, no. 4 (Leningrad, 1958).

Zinger, M. E., Osnovnye zakony po krainemu severu: pravo na poliarnye prostranstva i organizatsiia organov upravleniia (Basic Laws Regarding the Far North: The Right to Polar Expanses and the Organization of Agencies of Administration) (Leningrad: izd-vo Glavsevmorsput, 1935).

ABOUT THE AUTHOR

William E. Butler is a member of the District of Columbia Bar and a Research Assistant at the Washington Center of Foreign Policy Research of the Johns Hopkins University School of Advanced International Studies, where he is engaged in a study relating to Soviet foreign policy and Soviet international law.

Mr. Butler's previous publications include translations of the RSFSR (Russian Republic) Family Code and the USSR Customs Code and the compilation of two full-length bibliographies on Soviet law and Soviet international law published by the Harvard Law School Library in 1965 and 1966. He has published articles, translations, and reviews in the *Harvard International Law Journal*, *Pennsylvania Bar Association Quarterly*, *Soviet Statutes and Decisions*, *World Affairs*, and *International Legal Materials* and has visited the Soviet Union three times.

Mr. Butler received his B.A. degree from the American University School of International Service, M.A. from the Johns Hopkins School of Advanced International Studies, and LL.B. from the Harvard Law School.